This irresistible collection of cloned recipes is the product of years of obsessive research by self-confessed junk-food addict Todd Wilbur. Big food manufacturers guard their recipes like the gold in Fort Knox, but Wilbur's dogged pursuit of taste-alike versions of his— and our—all-time favorites has paid off in this unique cookbook of 50 scrumptious treats. Whether you're a kid or just a kid at heart, you'll have a great time making the incredible clones of a McDonald's® Big Mac®, a Burger King® Whopper®, a Tastykake® Butterscotch Krimpet®; a Yoo Hoo® Chocolate Drink, and all the other famous foods. Helpful illustrations let you recreate them to perfection. And both taste and guilty pleasures are just like the real thing!

TODD WILBUR has spent the last five years in his kitchen, testing the recipes for this book. He devotes the rest of his time to persuading others to taste his concoctions. He says his idea of the perfect Thanksgiving dinner is a "Big Mac and large fries." He lives in Emmaus, Pennsylvania.

Todd
Wilbur

RECIPES

CREATING KITCHEN
CLONES OF AMERICA'S
FAVORITE BRAND-
NAME FOODS

ILLUSTRATED BY THE AUTHOR

A PLUME BOOK

PLUME

Published by the Penguin Group
Penguin Books USA Inc., 375 Hudson Street, New York, New York 10014, U.S.A.
Penguin Books Ltd, 27 Wrights Lane, London W8 5TZ, England
Penguin Books Australia Ltd, Ringwood, Victoria, Australia
Penguin Books Canada Ltd, 10 Alcorn Avenue, Toronto, Ontario, Canada M4V 3B2
Penguin Books (N.Z.) Ltd, 182–190 Wairau Road, Auckland 10, New Zealand

Penguin Books Ltd, Registered Offices:
Harmondsworth, Middlesex, England

First published by Plume, an imprint of Dutton Signet,
a division of Penguin Books USA Inc.

First Printing, June, 1993

19 20 18

Text and illustrations copyright © Todd Wilbur, 1993
All rights reserved

 REGISTERED TRADEMARK—MARCA REGISTRADA

LIBRARY OF CONGRESS CATALOGING IN PUBLICATION DATA
Wilbur, Todd.
Top secret recipes : creating kitchen clones of America's favorite
brand-name foods / Todd Wilbur.
p.   cm.
ISBN 0-452-26995-4
1. Cookery, American.   2. Junk food.   I. Title.
TX715.W6586   1993
641.5973 — dc20   92-38670
CIP

Printed in the United States of America
Set in Gill Sans and Machine

Designed by Steven N. Stathakis

*To Trish
and my family,
for whom there
are no substitutes*

C O N T E N T S

A LITTLE FOREWORD

In the laboratory (my kitchen), each of these recipes was subjected to a battering array of bakings and mixings, batch after batch, until the closest representation of the actual commercial product was finally achieved. I did not swipe, heist, bribe, or otherwise obtain any formulas through coercion or illegal means. I'd like to think that many of these recipes are the actual formulas for their counterparts, but there's no way of knowing for sure. In such cases of closely guarded secret recipes, the closer one gets to matching a real product's contents, the less likely it is that the protective manufacturer will say so.

The objective here was to match the taste and texture of the products with everyday ingredients. In most cases, obtaining the exact ingredients for these mass-produced food products is nearly impossible. For the sake of security and convenience, many of the companies have contracted confidentially with vendors for the specialized production and packaging of each of their product's ingredients. These prepackaged mixes and ingredients are then sent directly to the company for final preparation.

Debbi Fields of Mrs. Fields Cookies, for example, arranged with several individual companies to custom manufacture many of her cookies' ingredients. Her vanilla alone is specially blended from a variety of beans grown in various places around the world. The other ingredients—the chocolate, the eggs, the sugars, the flour—all get specialized attention specifically for the Mrs. Fields company. The same holds true for McDonald's, Wendy's, KFC, and most of the big-volume companies.

Even if you could bypass all the security measures and somehow get your hands on the secret formulas, you'd have a hard time executing the recipes without locating many ingredients usually impossible to find at the corner market. Therefore, with taste in mind, substitution of ingredients other than those that may be used in the actual products is necessary in many cases to achieve a closely cloned end result.

INTRODUCTION

In 1987 I received in the mail a recipe with a letter attached, claiming it was the secret formula for Mrs. Fields Chocolate Chip Cookies. The sheet looked like a fifth- or sixth-generation photocopy. It told a curious story that went something like this: A woman had called the Mrs. Fields office in Park City, Utah, and requested the recipe for chocolate chip cookies. Someone at the office agreed to provide the recipe but told the woman it would cost her $2.50. The woman placed the fee on her credit card, and when she received her statement, was startled to see a charge for $250! She was so upset about the loss that she started a chain-letter campaign, sending out dozens of copies of the recipe to friends and family members, and encouraging them to do the same.

It didn't take long to realize that this wasn't actually the recipe for Mrs. Fields Cookies, much less a recipe that even came close to the original. So what was it then? Someone's idea of a really bad prank? Or perhaps something much more devious? Whatever the reason, someone was working hard at getting this chain-letter recipe into mailboxes all over the country, and I had become one of the lucky recipients.

I would later discover that this bogus recipe had been spreading quickly across the country. And the effects of this seemingly innocent chain letter were spelling out big problems for the Mrs. Fields company.

People who had tried the recipe were disillusioned by the finished product—a cookie that did not taste at all like a Mrs. Fields cookie but more like the desk coaster I set my coffee on. And the chain letter gave the impression that the company was in the business of selling its recipe—a claim that's simply not true. Some people even responded by accusing the firm of mistreating the woman caller.

It took the company a long time to overcome the adverse effects of the chain letter. Prominent signs were placed inside each store discrediting the recipe. You may have seen them. The cookie company never did discover the chain letter's creator or the motive behind it.

Fortunately for the company, today the incident is only a bad memory. But I remained inspired by the popularity of the recipe. Thousands had seen it and passed it on, feeling privy to this "secret" that they wanted to share. Too bad they were misled.

With all of this in mind, I focused on the recipe and wondered what it might take, aside from common kitchen sense, to make the recipe a little better, more like the original; to make the cookie soft and chewy in the center but crispy around the edges; to produce that deep buttery-vanilla aroma that lures customers away from their mall shopping over to the Mrs. Fields cookie counter. What would have to change to make it taste like the original cookies that Americans can't seem to pass up? In time, with a little trial and error and flour in the eye, I had come up with a cookie that tasted just like Mrs. Fields'—it was delicious! My kitchen cloning craze had begun, and that was the day this book was born.

Within these pages you will find recipes that will help you create home clones of very well known, well respected products. But don't mistake these recipes for the actual product formulas. They probably aren't. They'll just taste like the real thing to you—if all goes well.

It may at first seem silly to spend time making any of these foods that you can simply run out and buy, but there's actually some logic at work here. For instance, there isn't one city in this country where one can buy everything in this book—many of the items are regional. And there are both economic and nutritional concerns that make this book a useful stoveside companion. These recipes will give you a degree of control you didn't have before. You can now determine for yourselves what goes into these world-famous foods and what doesn't. You'll have control over when to make the food. You'll no longer be at the mercy of slow cooks, lines, or closed doors. And you'll have something to do on rainy days when video games start to cross your eyes and blister your firing thumb.

There is a sense of satisfaction that comes from creating something in your own kitchen that tastes just like a product that has tickled the taste buds of millions. Even more exciting are the expressions of amazement from others who taste your creations—"You made this?" Humbly nod and share the recipe.

True, nothing can absolutely replace the authentic creations that have proven themselves to consumers over time. But there are some very concrete and detailed reasons why your next culinary experiment should come from these pages.

COST

With today's changing economic conditions, Americans are watching their money ever more closely. Now, instead of going out to the store or fast-food restaurant for snacks and meals, a growing number of "frugal gourmets" are staying in the household kitchen, where food can be prepared in a healthier and more cost–effective way.

At 1992 prices a McDonald's Big Mac sells for about $1.90. If you were to make four Big Macs at home, this would be your expense list:

1	package (8) sesame-seed buns	$1.09
1	pound ground beef	1.45
1	head of lettuce	.89
1	white onion	.25
1	12-ounce bottle Kraft dressing	1.59
16	slices American cheese	2.09
1	16-ounce jar pickle slices	1.29
	TOTAL	$8.65

Considering that four real Big Macs cost $7.60 to our $8.65, the economics of the home burger begin to look unfavorable. But let's not forget that after making your four burgers, you'd still have bonus food left over.

You'd be left with:

> 4 sesame-seed buns
> ¾ head of lettuce
> ¾ white onion
> 10 ounces Kraft dressing
> 12 slices American cheese
> About 45 pickle slices

So all you'd need to buy for your next four burgers would be:

> 1 pound ground beef $1.45

Here's where the figures begin to come way down. Starting from scratch, if we average the numbers, eight Big Mac–style hamburgers will cost you only $1.40 apiece. That's a savings of $4.00 over buying them at the restaurant, or the equivalent of two free hamburgers and change. Plus, you'd *still* have half a head of lettuce, half an onion, two-thirds of a bottle of dressing, eight slices of American cheese, and thirty to forty sliced pickles left over.

And, as is usually the case with larger-volume production, your savings would be even more substantial if you made twelve hamburgers. Each of these sandwiches would cost you a measly $1.14, saving you a total of more than $9.00 over the retail price. That's like getting four free hamburgers and more than a dollar in change. Plus you'd *still* have lettuce, onion, dressing, cheese, and lots of pickles. At sixteen burgers you'd save close to 50 percent over the Mc-Donald's price.

This cost-savings analysis can be applied to most of the products in the book with similar results. In fact, there's hardly an item in this book that will not cost less to produce yourself than to purchase. Perhaps you're even lucky enough to have all the ingredients for a recipe on hand, creating a currently cost-free situation, much to your satisfaction and glee.

AVAILABILITY

In the fall of 1990 I moved from California to the East Coast, leaving behind some of the local goodies I had grown to crave from time to time. The original In-N-Out Double-Double hamburger, Carl's Jr., and Jack-in-the-Box sandwiches were now all out of reach. But with this book, and some time in the kitchen, clones that quench those cravings are just minutes away.

If you live east of the Mississippi, you've no doubt enjoyed Tastykake products. The brand's popularity in the region attests to that. If you leave the area, though, you're out of luck. Tastykake has a very limited distribution, and the only way you can enjoy a fresh Tastykake treat anywhere else is to have someone send it to you. Unless you've got a recipe.

Or maybe it's raining outside, and you're dying for some Reese's Peanut Butter Cups or a Twinkie. You can get these snacks just about anywhere. But you've got a crackling fire warming the house, a great episode of *Lost in Space* on the tube, and all the ingredients handy in your kitchen. So you tie on the apron and whip up your own. It's easy, it's fresh, and you don't have to comb your hair or put on your shoes.

INGREDIENTS

Whoever first said that a Twinkie has the shelf life of uranium was wrong. After being tucked away for a few years in the darkest, most forgotten abyss of your pantry, the spongy, filled snack cake will begin to resemble a huge potato bug. At that time, eating it is highly discouraged.

Yes, Twinkies are made to sit on the store shelves for a good length of time without going stale. Consumer confidence in the manufacturer weighs heavily on the product's freshness (or appearance thereof). As with thousands of products on grocery-store shelves, brand loyalty was won over with the additives that give your favorite snack its consistent texture, color, and taste from super-market to supermarket.

The use of additives in food dates back to 1859, when Sir William Henry Perkins found that coal-tar oil could be used to give many foods a mauve tint that was more appealing to buyers and that, coincidentally, matched the decor in some homes. The potentially harmful practice lasted some fifty years, until Teddy Roosevelt passed the Food & Drug Act in 1906, which banned many of the coal-tar dyes on the grounds that the American people were "being steadily poisoned by the dangerous foods that were being added to food with reckless abandon," according to the Department of Agriculture.

Granted, this is not the early 1900s, and many of the additives in today's foods have been proven safer than coal tar. But some 2,000 chemical additives are in use today, and the safety of some of them is still unclear. So ask yourself, "Am I a gambler?" If you eat lots of foods with chemical additives, you can bet you are.

With this book, not only will you be able to avoid the additives and preservatives that make your food sound like a lab experiment, you will also have the freedom to substitute ingredients to your heart's desire. Now you can replace the ground beef in your favorite hamburgers with ground turkey—a substitution that, according to The *Wall Street Journal,* is already being considered by some of the largest fast-food chains. (Is there a McGobble Burger in our future?) Or you may want to use a low-calorie sweetener in place of the sugar. Or get creative and make your own original peanut-butter-and-jelly-filled Twinkies. The substitutions and variations are only limited by your imagination . . . and your courage.

CURIOSITY AND CREATIVE FULFILLMENT

Most people never considered it possible to make a Twinkie in the kitchen or taste the twin of a Big Mac they slapped together at home in less than ten minutes. You hold the proof.

As you cook, you will find that most of these recipes taste

exactly like, or extremely similar to, their manufactured counterparts. I say *most* of the recipes, because:

1. Taste is an opinion subject to individual preference, and the memory of a particular taste can vary from person to person. One person might say that a hamburger tastes just like a Big Mac while another might think it ain't even close. Putting the *Top Secret Recipes* version right next to an original Big Mac, however, should help establish a consensus on the similarity.

2. Although the success of the fast-food concept lies in the security of consistency the customer receives from outlet to outlet, products created at different locations (especially franchises) are not always created equal. I've probably had four different versions of Wendy's chili—some with bigger chunks of meat, some with more onion, some spicier, some runnier.

These large companies attempt to idiot-proof their products as much as possible. While Wendy's chili is a great receptacle for the company's beef patties that break or do not sell, it is made by a kitchen chef following a recipe similar to the one in this book. In the haste of cooking for a lunch crowd, inconsistencies are not uncommon, with this or any other such designed menu item.

Developing a reasonable facsimile of a particular food depends on finding a common thread between all versions and replicating it. The recipes in this book are based on random samplings. They do not account for employee miscalculations in cooking or a manufacturer's later change in makeup of the product, nor do they account for variations in cooking time based on gas and electric ranges, or adjustments that need to be made in varying altitudes.

Although ingredient substitutions and experimentation are encouraged, you will create a more accurate clone of the original by using the exact ingredients specified and following the steps carefully.

But most of all, realize that this is a book created for enjoyment's sake, to give us fun alternatives to the foods we've made in the past.

Okay, so it may not be a book for some of the lazy snack lovers out there who feel cooking should be no more difficult than knowing how to set the timer on a microwave. But I'm convinced that most of you are of the breed motivated by the true snack lover's credo: This stuff tastes a heck of a lot better when it's fresh.

I understand that most of these recipes as written won't win a contest for nutritional awareness from the Pritikin Foundation. As health conscious as we may or may not claim to be, when our own inner Pavlov rings the bell, we're suddenly put on a mission commanded by Captain Taste Buds. That's when we walk barefoot over broken glass to satisfy the deep call for a Snickers bar. All pain and suffering is soothed by the palatal elation produced by the brand we've come to call our own, whether it's Twinkies or Snickers or a Big Mac.

So enjoy the recipes within these pages. Experiment and have fun with them.

I enjoyed writing this book, because I believe in adulation. And if what they say is true—that "imitation is the sincerest form of flattery"—then I've just paid some very big companies a darn good compliment or two.

CONVENIENCE FOOD:
AN AMERICAN LOVE AFFAIR

It appears that our exposure to fast foods and snack foods has generated a notorious love/hate relationship. Major fast-food chains are opening new stores at the rate of nine a week and scooping up $70 billion a year of Americans' hard-earned cash. Our country consumes more than 3 billion pounds of candy a year; that's an average of 17 pounds per person. And while sales of snack cakes, soda, ice cream, and other sweets rise all the time, so does enrollment in Nutri-System® and Jenny Craig™.

How much we love this stuff can be clearly seen in the advertising barrage constantly reminding us that we want and need more. Escaping the media blitz is impossible if you spend any time aboveground. How do you ignore a giant corporation like Mc-Donald's that spends more than $1 billion on advertising each year? Even if you don't succumb to the messages, you'll still find yourself humming the catchy jingles in the shower. Yes, we do deserve a break today.

The former chief nutritionist of New York City's Mount Sinai School of Medicine calls us "The McDonald's Generation." A popular and expensive advertising campaign refers to us as "The Pepsi Generation." Whatever you tag it, there's no disputing the fact that we are a generation of consumers that has come to appreciate and expect predictable quality from store to store, while embracing speed and convenience.

The sixty-one grams of fat in a Double Whopper with Cheese is going to sit like a lump in your belly until dinnertime, but when you're late for class or a one o'clock appointment, the Burger King drive-thru window is a quick and easy way to quiet a growling stomach. The advertising campaign for Snickers, America's number-one candy bar, appeals to just that sense of urgency and emptiness.

A catchy jingle claims that the special blend of peanuts, caramel, and nougat, all coated with milk chocolate, will easily appease our hunger—"Snickers satisfies you." Sure, it'll stop the hunger, but we'll be left with a nutritional black hole.

The truth is, when we have an urge to graze, fulfillment is king, nutrition a pawn. Since we were children we've been conditioned to ignore nutritional value and to crave the sweet, chewy, creamy satisfaction that comes from sugar- and oil-pumped foods. At the dinner table we were told that we couldn't have dessert until all our dinner was gone. And that's what got us through the Brussels sprouts—certainly not because we liked them.

"People do not eat foods because they are good for them— rather because they appeal to their appetite, to their emotions, to their soul," wrote Dr. Robert S. Harris, professor of nutritional bio- chemistry at the Massachusetts Institute of Technology. Let's face it, food is one of the most powerful emotional stimuli in our lives.

In his *Complete Junk Food Book*, Michael S. Lasky states, "Be- havioral psychologists tell us that flavor is probably the most im- portant characteristic in satisfying our appetites—the instinctive craving. The flavors we like best are not necessarily found in those foods that form part of a well-balanced, nutritious diet. We seem to be born junk food junkies. Well, not quite. But we are ideal candidates for the blitz of external brainwashing stimuli that will convince us the sweetened, the oily, and the salted provide the greatest pleasure."

When we satisfy our cravings with goodies like those found in this book, we practically get high on the oral gratification—much as we did when we were nursing infants, or when we were kids, and our parents treated us to a drive down to the local hamburger joint on a Saturday night.

Convenience foods are as popular as ever and will probably remain so. But the foods our taste buds guided us to in the past are now being reevaluated by our brains. An evolving nutritional aware- ness is altering fast-food menus to include more health-conscious fare. Salad bars, extra-lean burgers, and lower-cholesterol ingredi- ents are in demand, and corporate fast-food giants are delivering. Of course they are. They'll do whatever it takes to ensure that we continue to spend an average of one out of every two of our restaurant dollars on their food.

After all, that's the American way.

ONCE UPON A TIME

Convenience products are a twentieth-century phenomenon. Their roots go back centuries, but most of our popular prepackaged sweets and made-to-order foods didn't gain much ground until the 1900s rolled around.

In the late nineteenth century the French first discovered a special process of canning foods using heat that would preserve them for a greater length of time. The method also made storage, sale, and shipping much easier.

Soon, large canneries spread from Europe into America during what would be called the Industrial Revolution. More factories were built to box, bottle, and bag varieties of fruits, grains, vegetables, meats, and spices that formerly were sold only in bulk.

Then today's popular brand names began to emerge: Milton Hershey was making chocolate, Clarence Birdseye was packaging precooked fruits and vegetables, the National Biscuit Company (now Nabisco) was making crackers and cookies, druggist Charles Pemberton was bottling Coca-Cola, and F. W. Rueckheim was perfecting his Cracker Jack caramel-coated popcorn.

It was also around that time that the German contribution to our fast-food concept took hold. Some say it was at the Chicago World's Fair—some say it was on Coney Island—that the first frankfurter was introduced. The beef sausage slapped into a custom-made bun and dressed up with mustard and sauerkraut was perfect for carry-out eating at sidewalk carts and at baseball games. American cartoonist Tad Dorgan supplied the weiner with a head, tail, and legs in one of his drawings, and it has been called a hot dog ever since.

During the First World War, new methods of packaging and preservation of food were developed to help supply the American armies in Europe. We began to see the emergence of restaurants that focused on quicker service than what people had become used to around the turn of the century. Joseph Monninger wrote in *American Heritage* magazine, "It may have started in 1921 at the Royce Hailey's Pig Stand in Dallas when drivers began pulling up for barbecue sandwiches. Doubtless it started with cars, a population pushing out of the cities into the suburbs, and a volume of business based on large production at minimal costs: hamburger factories with retail outlets."

The hot dog begat the hamburger.

Later that year, in Wichita, Kansas, a bright man named E. W. Ingram opened his first restaurant. His concept was to sell steam-broiled hamburgers by the sack for five cents apiece. The concept caught on quickly. Some years later, Ingram's White Castle stores had spread into eleven other states.

The dawn of the automobile age gave birth to other successful drive-in restaurants. In 1922 Roy Allen and Fred White lent the initials of their last names to the first of the A&W root beer outlets. In 1925 Howard Johnson bought a money-losing drugstore, where he served his homemade ice cream at the soda fountain. Eventually he added hot dogs and hamburgers to the menu. When he began to turn a profit, he turned the store into a restaurant and expanded into other regions. Howard Johnson's was the first to establish the mass-market menu. And thus the fast-food chain was born.

It was during World War II that Americans found an even bigger need for convenience foods. The military required food that could be carried in small lightweight packages and that could be prepared and eaten easily. Advances were made in food freezing, dehydration, and fabrication. Vending machines were developed, and central commissaries provided mass-produced food. Supermarkets began to fill with greater numbers of packaged products, and fast-food restaurants—both drive-up and self-service—were multiplying.

By the end of the war, candy companies such as Hershey, Mars, Peter Paul, and Nestlé were all well established and putting smiles on the faces of millions of chocolate lovers. The snack-cake companies that produced the Hostess and Tastykake lines were enjoying huge success, while cookie and cracker manufacturers Keebler, Na-

TOP-SELLING CHOCOLATE BARS IN THE U.S.

RANK	CANDY	MANUFACTURER
1	Snickers	Mars
2	Reese's Peanut Butter Cups	Hershey
3	M&M's Peanut	Mars
4	M&M's Plain	Mars
5	Kit Kat	Hershey
6	Hershey's Almond	Hershey
7	Hershey's Milk Chocolate	Hershey
8	Milky Way	Mars
9	Butterfinger	Nabisco
10	Nestlé Crunch	Nestlé

bisco, and Pepperidge Farm were busy developing new products to boost their growing businesses.

In the forties, two Americans hungry for thicker wallets set out to satisfy the hunger of others. Carl Karcher and Glen Bell started their careers in convenience food in much the same way—each by selling hot dogs in southern California. They had witnessed the success of earlier quick-service start-up shops such as Dairy Queen, Orange Julius, and the White Tavern Shoppes (which would later become Long John Silver's Seafood Shoppes). They would each move into selling hamburgers and eventually find tremendous success in the fast-food industry, Karcher with his Carl's Jr. hamburger outlets and Bell with Mexican-style fast food at Taco Bell.

When these two first started flipping burgers, just around the corner were two brothers doing some flipping of their own. The brothers never thought these humble beginnings would give birth to a chain making the single biggest impact on American convenience food and marketing. Dick and Mac McDonald would see theirs become a household name.

It seems odd that today the McDonald's Corporation celebrates Founder's Day in honor of Ray Kroc, who died in 1984. The McDonald brothers had sold twenty-one restaurant franchises and had opened nine restaurants in California when Ray Kroc was still a

Chicago-based milkshake-machine salesman. It was only in 1954 that Kroc entered the picture. His curiosity had been aroused when the brothers ordered eight milkshake machines for their growing enterprise. No other restaurant needed to make that many milkshakes at once. So Kroc went to California to investigate. What he saw he liked. And wanted.

Kroc pressured the brothers to let him in on their success. A year later he became a franchisor with his first restaurant in Des Plaines, Illinois. Six years after that, Kroc convinced the brothers to sell their shares to him and his associates for $2.7 million—not much when you consider that McDonald's now has sales averaging $50 million a day.

It was Kroc who perfected what came to be known as "the system," for ensuring consistent, dependable service from outlet to outlet. But it was Dick and Mac McDonald who had the vision to replace the carhops that were widely used at drive-in hamburger stands at that time. It was the brothers who drew the layout of their new self-service concept in chalk on a tennis court and who would knock service time down from twenty minutes to twenty seconds. It was the brothers who decided to start using plastic utensils instead of metal and to serve the meal on paper plates and in bags.

"Up until the time we sold, there was no mention of Kroc being the founder," the surviving brother, eighty-two-year-old Dick McDonald, told the *Wall Street Journal.* "If we had heard about it, he would have been back selling milkshake machines." McDonald says today that the company history begins in 1955, "and everything before that is wiped out."

Another huge chain that was developing at the same time would compete with McDonald's for the number-one spot in fast food. Harland Sanders, christened a Kentucky colonel by the state governor, had set out across the country to share his secret blend of herbs and spices with restaurant owners for a small royalty on each piece of chicken they sold. His "finger lickin' good" recipe was a hit.

But in 1964 Sanders made a deal with some Nashville businessmen that he would later regret, much as the McDonald brothers did after making their deal with Kroc. Jack C. Massey and John Brown, Jr., convinced Sanders to sell the rights to his product for $2 million. In the contract, the Colonel was obligated to travel around the world over a quarter of a million miles a year as a PR man for the company—its human trademark. This made Sanders angry. But what bothered him most was that with the company out of his control, his recipes were being altered, such as the one for his tasty gravy —and there was nothing he could do about it. Just seven years later, Massey and Brown sold Kentucky Fried Chicken to Heublein, a liquor and food conglomerate, for $275 million. The Colonel had been deep-fried.

In the seventies women's move from the home into the office made convenience food even more of an American fixation. As a growing number of Moms joined Dads in the work force, there was less time for cooking. Families could depend on their local burger joint to sell them security. A sandwich bought today would taste like one bought yesterday, from location to location.

Grocery stores and supermarkets were tuned in to this appetite for speed and convenience. More items were hitting the shelves that took less or no time to prepare. One-step TV dinners were a big hit in the fifties and sixties. Then microwave ovens came along, and manufacturers had another million-dollar market open up wide for them.

Today there are 160,000 fast-food restaurants in the United States. McDonald's is the country's largest owner of real estate, and one person out of five eats at a fast-food restaurant on an average day, according to *Consumer Reports.*

Convenience stores can be found on every other corner, and supermarkets stock more than 11,000 items, many of which are backed by expensive advertising campaigns and packaged in containers that are their own billboards. Marketing studies quoted in Michael Lasky's *The Complete Junk Food Book* show that "70 to 90 percent of the time the purchase of such junkie favorites as candy, cookies, snacks, and frozen desserts is the result of an in-store decision. As it happens, they are all products with high profit margins."

High profit margins are typical of convenience food. Fast-food restaurants usually mark up their products by about 400 percent over cost: A hamburger that costs you $2.00 at the pick-up window costs only around 50 cents to make. Fast food is not always cheap

LEADING FAST-FOOD CHAINS IN THE U.S.

1991 RANKING	COMPANY	UNITS	1991 SALES in $ millions
1	McDonald's	12,418	19,928.2
2	Burger King	6,409	6,200.0
3	KFC	8,480	6,200.0
4	Pizza Hut	9,000	5,300.0
5	Hardee's	3,727	3,431.0
6	Wendy's	3,804	3,223.6
7	Taco Bell	3,670	2,800.0
8	Domino's Pizza	5,500	2,400.0
9	Dairy Queen	5,329	2,352.4
10	Little Caesars	3,650	1,725.0
11	Arby's	2,500	1,450.0
12	Subway	6,106	1,400.0
13	Dunkin' Donuts	2,203	990.8
14	Jack-in-the-Box	1,089	978.0
15	Baskin-Robbins	3,533	829.7
16	Carl's Jr.	630	614.0
17	Long John Silver's Seafood	1,450	555.0
18	Popeye's Fried Chicken	808	540.2
19	Sonic Drive-Ins	1,112	518.0
20	Church's Chicken	1,136	506.6
21	Captain D's	636	420.8
22	Chick-fil-A	460	324.6
23	TCBY	1,850	321.0
24	Round Table Pizza	575	320.0
25	Whataburger	475	318.4

SOURCE: *Restaurants & Institutions*

food. You will undoubtedly pay less for the same food you buy at the drive-thru if you make it yourself. Yes, convenience is gonna cost you.

What'll cost you even more is healthy convenience. KFC's Skin-Free Crispy chicken introduced in 1991 costs nearly 20 percent more than its greasier predecessor. TastyLights Creme Filled Cup Cakes, which are 94 percent fat free, cost 10 cents more a box than the regular Tastykake version. Hostess Twinkies Lights Low Fat Snack Cakes cost 60 cents more a box than regular Twinkies—that means you pay close to 25 percent more a box. There appears to be a new-math formula these days that applies to the healthier line of foods: Less costs more.

A new trend emerged in 1989, when an Omaha businessman named Phil Sokolof began running full-page ads in major newspapers denouncing the saturated-fat content of McDonald's food. Those ads echoed the concerns of a public whose chant—"We are what we eat"—was growing louder. In 1990 it had an effect. McDonald's and Wendy's switched from beef fat to vegetable oil for cooking french fries and hash browns. Other fast-food restaurants soon followed suit.

The move toward healthier fare spread through the world of convenience food. Soon we were seeing more grilled and roasted chicken sandwiches, leaner milkshakes, nonfat yogurt, bran muffins, side salads, lighter mayonnaise, baked potatoes, and the heralded McLean Deluxe—McDonald's 91 percent fat-free hamburger. There's even a new candy bar that's easier on the fat and calories, called Milky Way II.

And when health-minded America led to ecology-minded America, McDonald's and other chains found themselves at the center of controversy again. A movement to discourage the use of Styrofoam cartons and other environmentally damaging materials for packaging succeeded in convincing convenience-food companies that using recycled materials was the only way to go.

These are smart companies. They know that the best way to make a buck is to keep the customer happy. Keep the bathrooms clean, give service with a smile, keep prices down, and most of all, avoid controversy. They also know that it's a good idea to introduce a lot of new products—new products that may include the next Dairy Queen Blizzard, which now outsells all other Dairy Queen products. Or it could be the next Egg McMuffin, which revolutionized breakfast out of the home. These companies hope to unveil new products that will grab hold of a customer's palate and wring the money right out of his or her wallet.

Of course, you'll get your losers. Nobody wanted KFC's Barbecued Ribs, or Carl's Jr.'s Chicken Fried Steak Sandwich. Even McDonald's McD.L.T. got canned. You can't say the American palate isn't honest. Just because we need a quick fix doesn't mean we'll continue buying snack food and fast food we don't like. There's too much out there to choose from. The menus get bigger, the lights on the LIMITED TIME ONLY signs get brighter, the supermarket aisles get longer, and the prices for all this convenience keep creeping higher and higher.

Certainly there's a multitude of newly inspired products to look forward to in our even faster-paced future. At fast-food outlets we'll likely see more chicken and turkey products and items with international roots customized for American taste buds. In snacks we'll see more "sequels" to already existing products as manufacturers develop lines that appeal to health-conscious, label-scanning eaters. All those huge corporations will wrestle with one another for market shares, for shelf space, and for our attention wherever a message can be relayed.

As advertising millions become billions, as national becomes global, it is hard not to see where the beef is. There's big money to be made in convenience food. It is an industry that bears responsibility for changing the way we live. What was once a world of home-cooked meals is now a world of prescribed and proven secret formulas.

This book is an occasion to combine the best of those two worlds.

AUNT JEMIMA
MAPLE SYRUP

☆   ♥   ☎   ✎   ✉   ✂   ☛

The year 1989 marked the 100th anniversary of the Aunt Jemima trademark. The name was conceived in 1889 by Chris Rutt while he was attending a vaudeville show and watching a New Orleans–style dance number performed to a jazzy tune called "Aunt Jemima." Rutt liked the music so much he stuck the name on his products. The maple syrup came along much later, in 1964, and is now the country's largest-selling syrup.

Today some folks tell the story of how their friends or relatives once met Aunt Jemima many years ago and how she was a kind and cordial woman. Little do they realize these people were fooled by a promotional campaign for the products back in the forties and fifties that used actresses traveling from town to town dressed up and acting like the "famous woman." There never really was an Aunt Jemima.

2 cups water
1 cup granulated sugar
2 cups dark corn syrup

¼ teaspoon salt
1 teaspoon maple flavoring

1. Combine the first four ingredients in a saucepan over medium heat.
2. Stir occasionally, until the mixture comes to a full boil. Let it boil for 7 minutes.
3. Turn the heat off and let the syrup cool for 15 minutes.
4. Add the maple flavoring and stir.
5. When completely cool, transfer the syrup to a covered plastic or glass container.

• MAKES 1 QUART

TIDBITS

For syrup with a butter flavor, just add 3 tablespoons of butter to the mixture before heating.

For a lighter syrup, use a sugar substitute instead of the granulated sugar.

The absence of natural maple syrup in this recipe is not unusual. In fact, there is no real maple syrup in any Aunt Jemima syrups.

•   •   •   •

BEN & JERRY'S HEATH BAR CRUNCH ICE CREAM

☆   ♥   ☎   ✎   ✉   ✂   ☛

When Ben Cohen and Jerry Greenfield first met in their seventh-grade gym class, they quickly became good friends. After college, the two decided they wanted to try their hand at selling ice cream. With $12,000 to invest, they moved from New York to Burlington, Vermont, where they purchased an abandoned gas station as the first location for their ice cream store.

After passing a five-dollar correspondence course on ice cream making from Pennsylvania State University and spending their life savings on renovating the gas station, the two were officially in the ice cream business. Ben and Jerry opened the doors to their first ice cream parlor in 1978. The pair's ice cream was such a big hit that they soon moved to a much larger facility. Today, just fifteen years after opening day, they produce more than 500,000 gallons of ice cream each month.

Heath Bar Crunch was one of the earliest flavors on the menu and is still the most popular of the thirty original chunky ice cream creations that made them famous.

5 Heath candy bars
3 eggs
1 cup granulated sugar

3 cups whipping cream
1½ cups half-and-half
3 teaspoons vanilla extract

1. Freeze the candy bars.
2. Beat the eggs by hand until fluffy.
3. Slowly beat in the sugar.
4. Add the cream, half-and-half, and vanilla and mix well.
5. Pour the mixture into an ice cream maker and freeze.

6. While the ice cream is freezing, place the frozen candy bars in a plastic bag and break them into small pieces with a knife handle.
7. When the ice cream is done, remove it from the ice cream maker and add the candy pieces. Mix well with a large spoon and store in the freezer.

• MAKES 1 QUART

TIDBITS

The real secret to Ben & Jerry's ice cream is its consistency. It is a thick and creamy ice cream developed with special equipment that keeps a great deal of air out of the mixture. The less air in the ice cream, the thicker the consistency. Therefore, you may find the above recipe fills your ice cream maker a little more than other ice cream recipes.

It's also important to get the right consistency of Heath bar chunks. Most of the candy bar should be crushed into crumbs, but stop breaking the candy when there are still several 1- and ½-inch chunks remaining.

I hope you enjoy experimenting with this recipe and that you try substituting other ingredients for the Heath bar chunks, just as Ben and Jerry have. Try Reese's Peanut Butter Cups, Oreo cookies, Kit Kat bars, Rollo cups, M&Ms, and chunks of raw cookie dough.

• • • •

BORDEN
CRACKER JACK

☆ ♥ ☎ ✎ ✉ ✂ ☛

In 1871 a German immigrant named F. W. Rueckheim came to Chicago with $200 in his pocket. He used all of his money to open a small popcorn shop in the city and started selling a sweet caramel- and molasses–coated popcorn confection. Rueckheim's big break came in 1893, when the treat was served at Chicago's first world's fair. From then on the popcorn's popularity grew enormously. In 1896 a salesman tasting the treat for the first time said, "That's a cracker jack," and the name stuck. Shortly after Cracker Jack's debut another customer commented, "The more you eat, the more you want," and that's still the slogan today.

In 1912 the Cracker Jack Company started adding toy surprises, ranging from small books to miniature metal toy trains. To date they have given away more than 17 billion toy surprises. In 1964 Borden, Inc. bought the Cracker Jack Company, and today the Cracker Jack division is the largest user of popcorn in the world, popping more than twenty tons of corn a day.

4 quarts popped popcorn
(or 1⅓ bags microwave popcorn)
1 cup Spanish peanuts
4 tablespoons (½ stick) butter

1 cup brown sugar
½ cup light corn syrup
2 tablespoons molasses
¼ teaspoon salt

1. Preheat the oven to 250°F.
2. Combine the popcorn and peanuts in a metal bowl or on a cookie sheet and place in the preheated oven.
3. Combine all of the remaining ingredients in a saucepan.
4. Stirring over medium heat, bring the mixture to a boil.
5. Using a cooking thermometer, bring the mixture to the hard-ball stage (260°–275°F, or the point at which the syrup, when dripped

into cold water, forms a hard but pliable ball). This will take about 20 to 25 minutes (or until you notice the mixture turning a slightly darker brown).

6. Remove the popcorn and peanuts from the oven and, working quickly, pour the caramel mixture in a fine stream over them. Then place them back in the oven for 10 minutes.

7. Mix well every five minutes, so that all of the popcorn is coated.

8. Cool and store in a covered container to preserve freshness.

• MAKES 4 QUARTS

•   •   •   •

BROWN & HALEY ALMOND ROCA

☆　♥　☎　✎　✉　✂　☛

Founded in 1914 by Harry Brown and J. C. Haley in Tacoma, Washington, the Brown & Haley Candy Company is one of the oldest confectioners in the country. In 1923 the company hit the jackpot when Harry Brown and the former cook from what would eventually become M&M/Mars, created a chocolate-coated butter candy, sprinkled with California almonds. They took the sweet to Tacoma's head librarian, and she named it *Almond Roca—roca* means "rock" in Spanish. In 1927 the two men decided to wrap the little candies in imported gold foil and pack them into the now-familiar pink cans to extend their shelf life threefold. In fact, because of the way the candy was packaged, it was carried by troops in World War II, the Korean War, the Vietnam War, and the Gulf War.

The Brown & Haley candy company is still housed in the former shoe factory that it has occupied since 1919. Almond Roca is so popular today that it can be found in sixty-four countries and is a market leader in Hong Kong, Singapore, Korea, Taiwan, the Philippines, and Japan. The company sells more than 5 million pounds of Almond Roca each year and is the United States's leading exporter of packaged confections.

1 cup (2 sticks) butter
1 cup granulated sugar
3 tablespoons water
1 teaspoon light corn syrup

1 cup finely chopped toasted
  almonds
1 cup milk-chocolate chips

1. Melt the butter in a saucepan.
2. Add the sugar, water, and corn syrup.

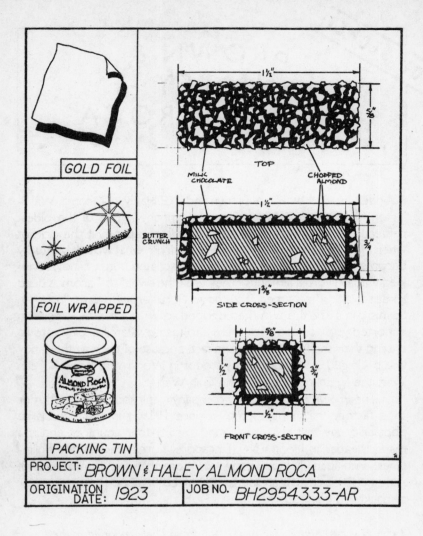

GOLD FOIL

FOIL WRAPPED

ALMOND ROCA

PACKING TIN

MILK CHOCOLATE

CHOPPED ALMOND

TOP

1½"

⅝"

BUTTER CRUNCH

1½"

3¾"

1⅜"

SIDE CROSS-SECTION

⅝"

½"

3¾"

½"

FRONT CROSS-SECTION

PROJECT: *BROWN & HALEY ALMOND ROCA*

ORIGINATION DATE: *1923*

JOB NO. *BH2954333-AR*

3. Cook the mixture over medium heat, stirring.
4. When the sugar dissolves and the mixture begins to boil, raise the heat and bring the mixture to 290°F on a cooking thermometer. (This is called the *soft-crack stage*.) It will be light brown in color, and syrup will separate into threads that are not brittle when dribbled into cold water.

5. Quickly stir in ½ cup chopped almonds.
6. Immediately pour the mixture onto an ungreased baking sheet.
7. Wait 2 or 3 minutes for the candy surface to firm, then sprinkle on the chocolate chips.
8. In a few minutes, when the chips have softened, spread the chocolate evenly over the surface.
9. Sprinkle the remaining almonds over the melted chocolate.
10. When the chocolate hardens, crack the candy into pieces. Store covered.

• MAKES 1 ½ POUNDS

Heath® bar or Hershey's® Skor®

These two candy bars are very similar, and both are composed of ingredients similar to those in Almond Roca. One obvious difference is that there are no almonds on top of these bars. To make these candy bars, simply follow the same directions for Almond Roca, omitting step 9.

TIDBITS

These recipes taste very much like the candies they clone, but you may notice right away that the finished products don't *look* like their corporate counterparts. This is largely due to the fact that the chocolate is only a top coating, surrounding the almond candy centers. This was done in the interest of simplicity—to make the recipes easier on the chef (that's you, right?). You could make your almond candy center first, then crack it into smaller pieces and dip those into chocolate. But is it really worth the trouble?

•   •   •   •

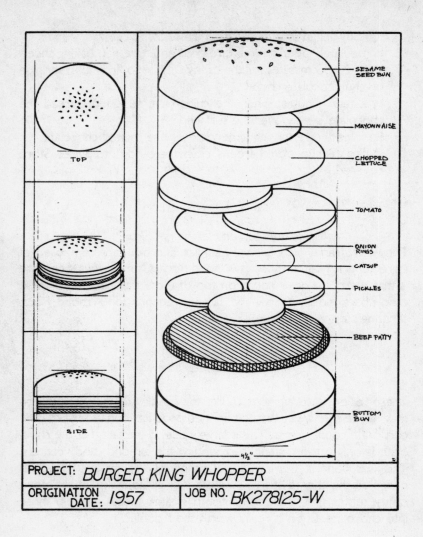

TOP

SIDE

SESAME SEED BUN

MAYONNAISE

CHOPPED LETTUCE

TOMATO

ONION RINGS

CATSUP

PICKLES

BEEF PATTY

BOTTOM BUN

4½"

PROJECT: *BURGER KING WHOPPER*

ORIGINATION DATE: *1957*

JOB NO. *BK278125-W*

BURGER KING
WHOPPER

☆　　♥　　☎　　✎　　✉　　✂　　☞

In 1954, in Miami, Florida, James McLamore and David Edgerton built the first Burger King Restaurant. By 1991 more than 6,400 Burger King outlets could be found in forty countries and all fifty states. That gives this burger giant more than $6 billion in sales each year, making it the country's second-largest fast-food chain. (McDonald's is the largest.)

For many, the favorite item on the menu is a flame-broiled hamburger conceived by the partners on a business trip from Orlando to Miami in 1957. Dubbed the "Whopper," this sandwich is overwhelmingly popular; figures show that Burger King sells more than 540 million annually, or nearly 2 million each day. And with more than 1,023 different combinations of the eight-or-so ingredients, including a vegetarian version, you really can "have it your way."

1 sesame-seed hamburger bun	3 to 4 onion rings
¼ pound ground beef	2 tomato slices
Dash salt	¼ cup chopped lettuce
3 dill pickle slices	1 tablespoon mayonnaise
1 teaspoon catsup	

1. Preheat a barbecue grill on high.
2. Toast both halves of the bun, face down, in a hot skillet. Set aside.
3. Form the beef into a thin patty slightly larger than the bun.
4. Lightly salt the hamburger patty and cook on the barbecue grill for 2 to 3 minutes per side.
5. Build the burger in the following stacking order from the bottom up:

bottom bun   tomatoes
hamburger patty   lettuce
pickles   mayonnaise
catsup   top bun
onion rings

• MAKES 1 HAMBURGER

TIDBITS

It's important that your barbecue grill be clean so that the hamburger will not pick up the taste of any food that was previously cooked there. Some foods, such as fish, are especially potent.

Also, be sure your grill is good and hot before cooking.

•   •   •   •

CARL'S JR.
FAMOUS STAR

☆ ♥ ☎ ✎ ✉ ✄ ☞

It was in Los Angeles in 1941 that Carl Karcher and his wife, Margaret, found a hot-dog cart on Florence and Central for sale for $326. They borrowed $311 on their Plymouth, added $15 of their own, and bought the brightly colored stand. Although the sign on this first stand read HUGO'S HOT DOGS, Karcher began purchasing more carts, painting on them CARL'S HOT DOGS. In 1945 Karcher opened his first drive-thru restaurant, which he named Carl's Drive-In Barbecue. In 1956 he opened two smaller restaurants in Anaheim and Brea, California, and used the Carl's Jr. name for the first time.

With 630 units as of 1991, the chain's trademark smiling star can be seen throughout the West and Southwestern United States, as well as in Mexico, Japan, and Malaysia. The chain has come a long way from the days when Karcher used to mix the secret sauce in twenty-gallon batches on his back porch. Carl's Jr. takes credit for introducing salad bars to fast-food restaurants back in 1977. Today, salads are regular fare at most of the major chains.

Carl's top-of-the-line hamburger is still the flame-broiled Famous Star, one of several products that has made Carl's Jr. famous.

1 sesame-seed hamburger bun	Dash salt
2 onion rings	2 teaspoons mayonnaise
½ teaspoon sweet pickle relish	3 dill pickle slices
1½ teaspoons catsup	¼ cup coarsely chopped lettuce
¼ pound ground beef	2 tomato slices

1. Preheat a clean barbecue grill on high. (The cleaner the barbecue, the less likely the beef patty will pick up other flavors left on the grill.)

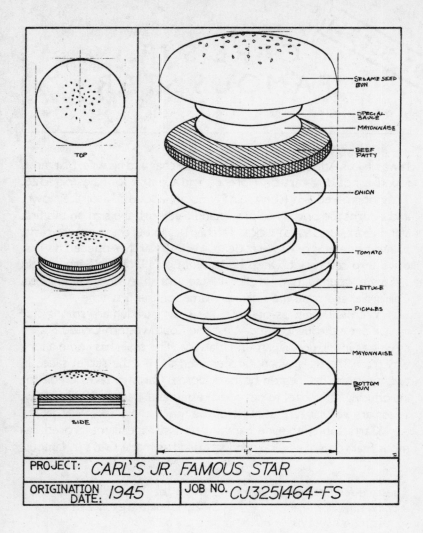

TOP

SIDE

SESAME SEED BUN

SPECIAL SAUCE

MAYONNAISE

BEEF PATTY

ONION

TOMATO

LETTUCE

PICKLES

MAYONNAISE

BOTTOM BUN

4"

PROJECT: CARL'S JR. FAMOUS STAR

ORIGINATION DATE: 1945

JOB NO. CJ3251464-FS

2. Toast both halves of the bun, face down, in a skillet over medium heat. Set aside.
3. Cut each of the 2 onion rings into quarters.
4. Mix the catsup and relish together. This is your "secret sauce."
5. Form the ground beef into a thin patty slightly larger than the bun.

6. Grill the meat for 2 or 3 minutes per side. Salt lightly.
7. Build the burger in the following stacking order from the bottom up:

bottom bun	beef patty
half of the mayonnaise	remainder of mayonnaise
pickles	special sauce (catsup and
lettuce	relish)
tomato slices	top bun
onion	

• MAKES 1 HAMBURGER

•   •   •   •

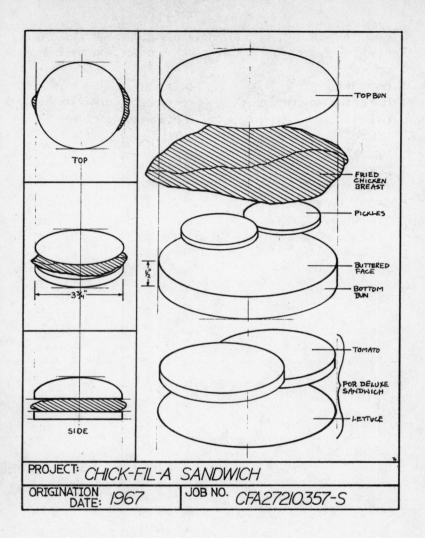

TOP

FRIED CHICKEN BREAST

TOP BUN

PICKLES

BUTTERED FACE

BOTTOM BUN

TOMATO

FOR DELUXE SANDWICH

LETTUCE

3¾"

½"

SIDE

PROJECT:	CHICK-FIL-A SANDWICH	
ORIGINATION DATE: 1967	JOB NO.	CFA27210357-S

36

CHICK-FIL-A CHICKEN SANDWICH

☆   ♥   ☎   ✎   ✉   ✂   ☛

In 1946 twenty-five-year-old S. Truett Cathy and his younger brother, Ben, opened a restaurant called The Dwarf House in Hapeville, Georgia. In the early sixties Cathy began experimenting with different seasonings and a faster cooking method for his original chicken sandwich. The finished product is the famous pressure-cooked chicken sandwich now served at all 460 Chick-fil-A outlets in thirty-one states.

Annual sales for the chain topped $324 million in 1991. That makes Chick-fil-A the fourth largest fast-food chicken restaurant in the world. And Cathy still adheres to the deeply religious values that were with him in the days of the first Dwarf House. That is why you won't find any Chick-fil-A restaurants open on Sundays.

3 cups peanut oil
1 egg
1 cup milk
1 cup flour
2½ tablespoons powdered sugar
½ teaspoon pepper

2 tablespoons salt
2 skinless, boneless chicken
    breasts, halved
4 plain hamburger buns
2 tablespoons melted butter
8 dill pickle slices

1. Heat the peanut oil in a pressure cooker over medium heat to about 400°F.
2. In a small bowl, beat the egg and stir in the milk.
3. In a separate bowl, combine the flour, sugar, pepper, and salt.
4. Dip each piece of chicken in milk until it is fully moistened.
5. Roll the moistened chicken in the flour mixture until completely coated.

6. Drop all four chicken pieces into the hot oil and close the pressure cooker. When steam starts shooting through the pressure release, set the timer for 3½ minutes.
7. While the chicken is cooking, spread a coating of melted butter on the face of each bun.
8. When the chicken is done, remove it from the oil and drain or blot on paper towels. Place two pickles on each bottom bun; add a chicken breast, then the top bun.

• MAKES 4 SANDWICHES

TIDBITS

It is very important that your oil be hot for this recipe. Test the temperature by dropping some of the flour coating into the oil. If it bubbles rapidly, your oil is probably hot enough. It should take about 20 minutes to heat up.

To make a "deluxe" chicken sandwich, simply add two tomato slices and a leaf of lettuce. Mayonnaise also goes well on this sandwich— it is a side order at the restaurant.

•   •   •   •

DAIRY QUEEN
BLIZZARD

☆   ♥   ☎   ✎   ✉   ✄   ☞

When the United States was emerging from the Great Depression in 1938, J. F. McCullough was experimenting with the idea of creating a new frozen dairy product. McCullough felt ice cream tasted better when it was soft and dispensed fresh from the freezer, not frozen solid. To test his theory with the public, McCullough held an "All-the-Ice-Cream-You-Can-Eat-for-Only-10-Cents" sale at a friend's ice cream store. More than 1,600 people were served the soft ice cream in the course of two hours. Convinced that the new product was a big hit, McCullough had to find a machine that could dispense the product at the right consistency. It wasn't long before he found Harry Oltz, the inventor of a freezer that could do the job. In 1940 McCullough opened the first Dairy Queen in Joliet, Illinois.

As of 1991 the company claimed to have more than 5,300 retail stores in the United States and twelve other countries. Since its creation in 1985, the Blizzard has shot to the top as the most popular Dairy Queen product, with more than 200 million of the treats sold each year. This is my version of the treat with Heath bar added.

1 Heath candy bar	2½ cups vanilla ice cream
¼ cup milk	1 teaspoon fudge topping

1. Freeze the Heath bar.
2. Break the candy into tiny pieces with a knife handle before removing from wrapper.
3. Combine all of the ingredients in the blender and blend for 30 seconds on medium speed. Stop the blender to stir the mixture with a spoon; repeat until well mixed.
4. Pour into a 16-ounce glass.

• MAKES 1 SERVING

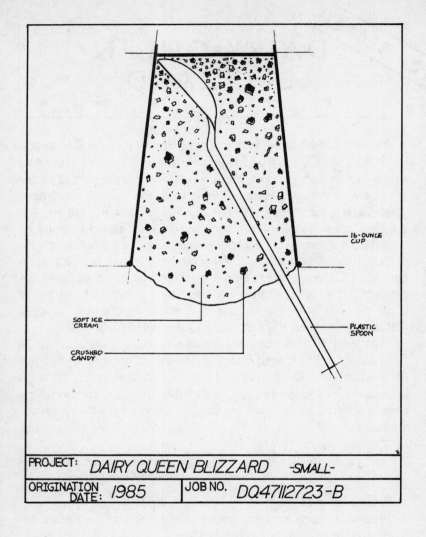

16-OUNCE
CUP

SOFT ICE
CREAM

CRUSHED
CANDY

PLASTIC
SPOON

PROJECT:	*DAIRY QUEEN BLIZZARD*	*-SMALL-*
ORIGINATION DATE: *1985*	JOB NO.	*DQ47112723-B*

TIDBITS

You can also make this treat with a variety of other candy ingredients. Some of the more popular Dairy Queen add-ins include pieces of Butterfinger candy bars, Reese's Peanut Butter Cups, and Oreo cookies. Now's your chance to be creative.

Also, corporate procedure dictates that when a customer is served a Blizzard in a Dairy Queen outlet, the server must turn the cup upside down quickly to confirm the thickness of the treat before handing it over. If everything is in order, the Blizzard won't "kerplop" onto the counter in front of you.

After using a conventional blender in this recipe (not a commercial mixer as found in Dairy Queens), your Blizzard may not be quite as thick as its commercial counterpart.

If you would like a thicker treat, after pouring the mixture into your cup, simply place it in the freezer for 5 to 10 minutes, or until it reaches the desired consistency. Then give it your own thickness test. Cross your fingers and turn the cup upside down. Have a towel handy.

•   •   •   •

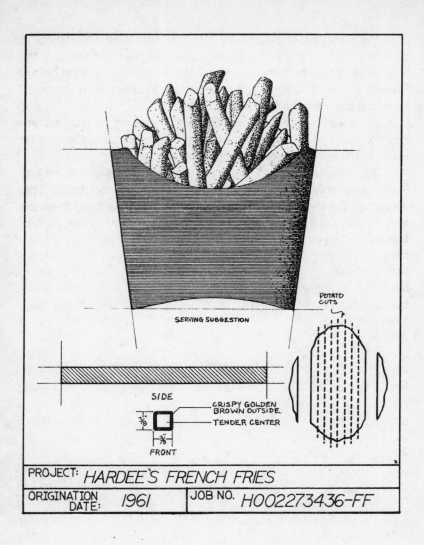

POTATO CUTS

SERVING SUGGESTION

SIDE

CRISPY GOLDEN BROWN OUTSIDE
TENDER CENTER

$\frac{3}{8}$"
$\frac{3}{8}$"

FRONT

PROJECT: HARDEE'S FRENCH FRIES

ORIGINATION DATE: 1961

JOB NO. H002273436-FF

HARDEE'S
FRENCH FRIES

☆　　♥　　☎　　✎　　✉　　✄　　☛

Led by CEO Leonard Rawls, the Hardee's Company opened its first hamburger restaurant in 1961 at the corner of Church Street and Falls Road in Rocky Mount, North Carolina. Hardee's has grown steadily through the years, with a number of well-planned acquisitions: first, the purchase of the 200-unit Sandy's chain in 1972, then the buyout of the 650-unit Burger Chef chain in 1983. The company's latest acquisition was the 1990 buyout of the 648 Roy Rogers restaurants. This latest purchase made Hardee's the third largest hamburger chain in the world, just behind McDonald's and Burger King. With that acquisition, the company claimed to be operating close to 3,800 restaurants in forty-one states and nine foreign countries.

Hardee's was the first major hamburger chain to switch to all-vegetable oil to cook its fried products. One of those products is french fries, the most popular item on the Hardee's menu.

6 cups vegetable oil
⅓ cup granulated sugar
2 cups warm water

2 large russett potatoes, peeled
Salt

1. Heat the oil in a deep saucepan over low-medium heat for about 20 minutes.
2. In a medium bowl, mix the sugar into the water until dissolved.
3. Cut the potatoes in half lengthwise, and then into ¼-inch strips.
4. Put the potatoes into the sugar solution and soak for 15 minutes.
5. Remove the potatoes and dry them thoroughly on paper towels.
6. The right oil temperature is crucial here. To test the oil, fry a couple of potato slices for 6 minutes. Remove and cool, then taste. The fries should not get too dark too soon and should be soft in the middle. If the oil is too hot, turn it down and test

again. The fries should not be undercooked, either. If they are, turn up the heat.

7. When the oil temperature is just right, put all of the potato slices in the oil for 1 minute. This is the blanching stage.
8. Take the fries out of the oil and let them cool.
9. When the fries have cooled, place them into the oil again for 5 minutes, or until golden brown.
10. Remove from the oil and place on a paper towel–covered plate.
11. Salt to taste.

• Makes 4 to 5 dozen french fries

TIDBITS

Oil temperature is crucial in cooking these french fries. Be sure to test the oil on several potato slices before cooking massive portions. And keep in mind that the more you cook at once, the longer your cooking time may be.

The blanching stage may seem to be a nuisance, but it is crucial if you want your fries to come out right. Blanching allows the fries to soak up a little oil while cooling, and will make them crispy when done.

•   •   •   •

HARDEE'S ¼-POUND HAMBURGER

☆　♥　☎　✎　✉　✂　☛

In 1975 Hardee's opened its 1,000th restaurant. The 2,000th unit was opened in 1983, and shortly after that, in 1988, the 3,000th unit opened its doors. This pattern of expansion has continued: A new Hardee's restaurant now opens on the average of one each workday. With the acquisition of the Roy Rogers chain in 1990, Hardee's neared the 4,000-unit mark, racking up systemwide sales of more than $3 billion. This is a chain that has come a long way since its first menu in 1961, which contained only eight items, including fifteen-cent hamburgers and ten-cent soft drinks.

As part of its continuing effort to offer nutrition-conscious customers a range of menu choices, Hardee's was one of the first of the "Big Four" burger chains to switch to low-calorie mayonnaise for its sandwiches.

1 sesame-seed hamburger bun	1 large tomato slice
¼ pound ground beef	1 leaf lettuce
Dash salt	1 teaspoon low-calorie
2 onion rings	mayonnaise
3 sliced dill pickles	1 teaspoon catsup

1. Preheat a griddle or frying pan to medium temperature.
2. Toast both halves of the hamburger bun, face down. Set aside.
3. Form the ground beef into a patty slightly larger than the bun. Salt it lightly.
4. Cook the patty for 2 to 3 minutes on each side.
5. Build the burger in the following stacking order from the bottom up:

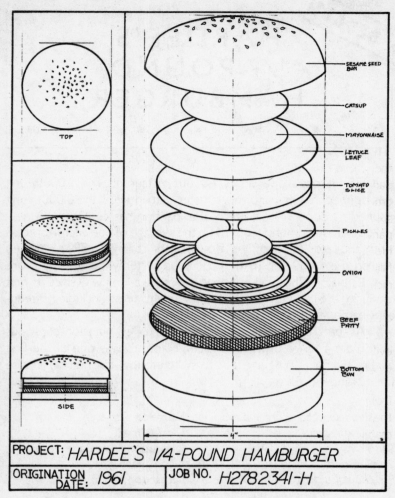

TOP

SIDE

SESAME SEED
BUN

CATSUP

MAYONNAISE

LETTUCE
LEAF

TOMATO
SLICE

PICKLES

ONION

BEEF
PATTY

BOTTOM
BUN

4"

PROJECT: *HARDEE'S 1/4-POUND HAMBURGER*

ORIGINATION DATE: *1961*   **JOB NO.** *H2782341-H*

bottom bun	lettuce leaf
beef patty	mayonnaise
onion rings	catsup
pickles	top bun
tomato slice	

• MAKES 1 HAMBURGER

• • • •

HOSTESS TWINKIE

☆ ♥ ☎ ✎ ✉ ✂ ☛

The Twinkie was invented in 1930 by the late James A. Dewar, then the Chicago-area regional manager of Continental Baking Company, the parent corporation behind the Hostess trademark. At the time, Continental made "Little Short Cake Fingers" only during the six-week strawberry season, and Dewar realized that the aluminum pans in which the cakes were baked sat idle the rest of the year. He came up with the idea of injecting the little cakes with a creamy filling to make them a year-round product and decided to charge a nickel for a package of two.

But Dewar couldn't come up with a catchy name for the treat—that is, until he set out on a business trip to St. Louis. Along the road he saw a sign for TWINKLE TOE SHOES, and the name TWINKIES evolved. Sales took off, and Dewar reportedly ate two Twinkies every day for much of his life. He died in 1985.

The spongy treat has evolved into an American phenomenon, from which nearly everyone has slurped the creamy center. Today the Twinkie is Continental's top Hostess-line seller, with the injection machines filling as many as 52,000 every hour.

You will need a spice bottle (approximately the size of a Twinkie), ten 12 × 14-inch pieces of aluminum foil, a cake decorator or pastry bag, and a toothpick.

CAKE
Nonstick spray
4 egg whites
One 16-ounce box golden pound
   cake mix
⅔ cup water

FILLING
⅓ cup vegetable shortening
1½ cups powdered sugar
1 tablespoon granulated sugar
⅓ cup cream
1 teaspoon vanilla extract
2 drops lemon extract

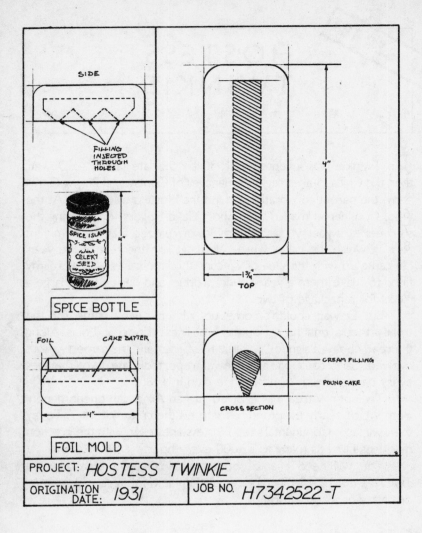

SIDE

FILLING INJECTED THROUGH HOLES

SPICE ISLAND
WHOLE
CELERY
SEED

4"

SPICE BOTTLE

FOIL   CAKE BATTER

4"

FOIL MOLD

4"

1¾"
TOP

CREAM FILLING

POUND CAKE

CROSS SECTION

PROJECT: *HOSTESS TWINKIE*

ORIGINATION DATE: *1931*

JOB NO. *H7342522-T*

1. Preheat the oven to 325°F.
2. Fold each piece of aluminum foil in half twice. Wrap the folded foil around the spice bottle to create a mold. Leave the top of the mold open for pouring in the batter. Make twelve of these molds and arrange them on a cookie sheet or in a shallow pan. Grease the inside of each mold with a light coating of nonstick spray.

3. Disregard the directions on the box of cake mix. Instead, beat the egg whites until stiff. In a separate bowl combine cake mix with water, and beat until thoroughly blended (about 2 minutes). Fold egg whites into cake batter, and slowly combine until completely mixed.
4. Pour the batter into the molds, filling each one about ¾ inch. Bake in the preheated oven for 30 minutes, or until the cake is golden brown and a toothpick stuck in the center comes out clean.
5. For the filling, cream the butter and shortening. Slowly add the sugars while beating.
6. Add the evaporated milk, vanilla, and lemon extract.
7. Mix on medium speed until completely smooth and fluffy.
8. When the cakes are done and cooled, use a toothpick to make three small holes in the bottom of each one. Move the toothpick around the inside of each cake to create space for the filling.
9. Using a cake decorator or pastry bag, inject each cake with filling through all three holes.

• MAKES 10

• • • •

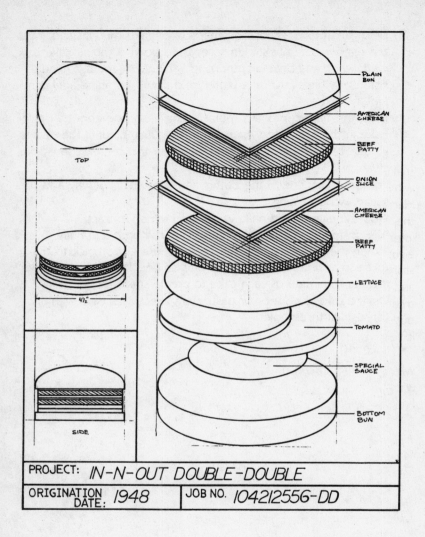

TOP

4½"

SIDE

PLAIN BUN

AMERICAN CHEESE

BEEF PATTY

ONION SLICE

AMERICAN CHEESE

BEEF PATTY

LETTUCE

TOMATO

SPECIAL SAUCE

BOTTOM BUN

PROJECT: *IN-N-OUT DOUBLE-DOUBLE*

ORIGINATION DATE: *1948*

JOB NO. *104212556-DD*

IN-N-OUT
DOUBLE-DOUBLE

☆   ♥   ☎   ✎   ✉   ✂   ☞

In 1948 Harry and Esther Snyder opened In-N-Out Burger in Baldwin Park, the first drive-thru restaurant in southern California. When Harry Snyder died in 1976, his son Richard took over the helm of the company, being sure to keep intact the simplicity that was so important to his father. The outlet still has a very small menu—only eight items. The french fries are made from fresh potatoes in each store, all the burgers are made to order, the lettuce is hand-leafed, and the milkshakes are made from fresh ice cream. All of this special treatment means that service is much slower than at most fast-food outlets—an average of twelve minutes per order. The experience is reminiscent of hamburger drive-ins of the fifties.

The company now has more than seventy-one outlets, each of which sells more than 52,000 hamburgers a month. Among these are the increasingly popular Double-Double hamburgers—quite a handful of sandwich.

1 plain hamburger bun	1 large lettuce leaf
1/3 pound ground beef	4 slices American cheese (singles)
Dash salt	OR 2 slices real American
1 tablespoon Kraft Thousand	cheese
Island dressing	1 onion slice
1 large tomato slice (or 2 small	
slices)	

1. Preheat a frying pan over medium heat.
2. Lightly toast both halves of the hamburger bun, face down. Set aside.
3. Separate the beef into two even portions, and form each half into a thin patty slightly larger than the bun.

4. Lightly salt each patty and cook for 2 to 3 minutes on the first side.
5. Flip the patties over and place two slices of cheese on top of each one. Cook for 2 to 3 minutes.
6. Build the burger in the following stacking order from the bottom up:

bottom bun   beef patty with cheese
dressing   onion slice
tomato   beef patty with cheese
lettuce   top bun

• MAKES 1 HAMBURGER

TIDBITS

The recipe requires 4 slices of cheese if you are using the common individually wrapped American cheese slices; also known as "cheese food." However, if you would like to use thicker, real American cheese slices, use only 1 slice on each beef patty.

•　　•　　•　　•

JACK-IN-THE-BOX JUMBO JACK

In 1950 a man named Robert O'Petersen built the first Jack-in-the-Box restaurant at El Cahon and 63rd streets in San Diego, California. The restaurant was originally built for drive-thru and walk-up service only—customers would speak into a clown's mouth to order their food. The clown was blasted to smithereens with explosives in a 1980 advertising campaign, however, signifying a shift toward a more diverse adult menu.

The Jumbo Jack hamburger has been on the menu since 1974.

1 sesame-seed hamburger bun	2 tomato slices
1/5 pound ground beef	1 large lettuce leaf
Dash salt	2 dill pickle slices
2 teaspoons mayonnaise	1 tablespoon chopped onion

1. Preheat a frying pan over medium heat.
2. Lightly toast both halves of the hamburger bun, face down. Set aside.
3. Form the ground beef into a thin patty slightly larger than the hamburger bun.
4. Cook the patty in the hot pan for 2 to 3 minutes per side. Lightly salt.
5. Build the burger in the following stacking order from the bottom up:

bottom bun
half of mayonnaise
beef patty
tomatoes
lettuce leaf

pickles
onion
remainder of mayonnaise
top bun

- MAKES 1 HAMBURGER

TIDBITS

If you want to add a slice of American cheese, it should go on top
of the beef patty.

•   •   •   •

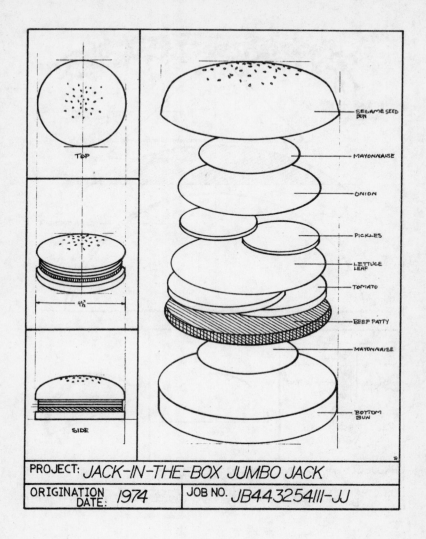

TOP

SIDE

4½"

SESAME SEED BUN

MAYONNAISE

ONION

PICKLES

LETTUCE LEAF

TOMATO

BEEF PATTY

MAYONNAISE

BOTTOM BUN

PROJECT: *JACK-IN-THE-BOX JUMBO JACK*

ORIGINATION DATE: *1974*

JOB NO. *JB443254III-JJ*

55

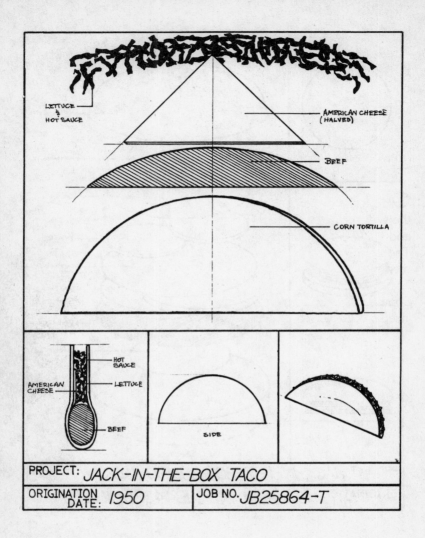

LETTUCE
&
HOT SAUCE

AMERICAN CHEESE
(HALVED)

BEEF

CORN TORTILLA

HOT SAUCE

AMERICAN CHEESE

LETTUCE

BEEF

SIDE

PROJECT: JACK-IN-THE-BOX TACO

ORIGINATION DATE: 1950

JOB NO. JB25864-T

JACK-IN-THE-BOX TACO

☆   ♥   ☎   ✎   ✉   ✂   ☞

Older than both McDonald's and Burger King, Jack-in-the-Box is the world's fifth-largest hamburger chain, with 1,089 outlets (by the end of 1991) in thirteen states throughout the West and Southwest. The restaurant, headquartered in San Diego, boasts one of the largest menus in the fast-food world—a whopping forty-five items.

Now taste for yourself the homemade version of Jack's most popular item. The Jack-in-the-Box Taco has been served since the inception of the chain, with very few changes over the years.

1 pound ground beef	12 soft corn tortillas
1/3 cup refried beans	3 cups cooking oil (Crisco brand
1/4 teaspoon salt	preferred)
2 tablespoons chili powder	6 slices American cheese
1/4 cup Ortega or Pico Pica brand	1 head finely chopped lettuce
mild taco sauce	

1. Slowly brown the ground beef over low heat, using a wooden spoon to chop and stir the meat, keeping it very fine and smooth.
2. When the beef is brown, drain the fat.
3. Add the refried beans and use the wooden spoon to smash the whole beans into the mixture, creating a smooth texture.
4. Add the salt, chili powder, and 2 tablespoons of the taco sauce to the mixture. Remove from the heat.
5. In another skillet, heat 1/4 inch of oil until hot. (Test with a small piece of tortilla—it should bubble when dropped into the oil.) Crisco oil will give the food a taste closest to the original.

6. Spread $\frac{1}{12}$ of the beef mixture on the center of each corn tortilla.
7. Fold the tortillas over and press so that the beef filling acts as an adhesive and holds the sides together.
8. Drop each taco into the pan of hot oil and fry on both sides until crispy.
9. When cooked, remove the tacos from the oil and place them on a rack or some paper towels until they are a little cooler.
10. Pry open each taco slightly. Add $\frac{1}{2}$ slice of American cheese (cut diagonally) and some lettuce. Top with about 1 $\frac{1}{2}$ teaspoons of the remaining taco sauce.

• MAKES 12 TACOS

TIDBITS

Try to use very thin tortillas for this recipe so that they won't crack when you fold the filled tacos in half before frying. It's best to use warm tortillas and even moisten them along the middle where you will be folding, for additional flexibility.

•   •   •   •

KAHLÚA COFFEE LIQUEUR

☆　♥　☎　✎　✉　✂　☛

No one knows for sure the true origin of Kahlúa, the largest-selling imported liqueur in America, but we do have a few clues. The oldest proof of Kahlúa's date of origin is a bottle found by Maidstone Co., a former distributor of the liqueur. The bottle came from Mexico, where the drink is now made, and is dated 1937. The word *Kahlúa* was discovered to have ties to ancient Arabic languages, and the old label, which bears a similarity to the current label, shows a turbaned man smoking a pipe beneath a Moorish archway. The only obvious change in the current label is that the man has become a sombrero-wearing Mexican napping beneath the same Moorish archway.

In 1959 Jules Berman discovered Kahlúa in Mexico and started importing it to the United States. In 1991 Kahlúa had annual world-wide sales of more than 2½ million cases, or the equivalent of 750 million drinks a year.

You will need an empty 750-ml. liquor bottle with a top for storing the liqueur.

2 cups water
1½ cups granulated sugar
1½ tablespoons instant coffee

2 cups 80-proof vodka
1½ tablespoons vanilla extract

1. Combine water, sugar, and coffee in a covered saucepan over high heat. Bring mixture to a boil, and continue to boil for 10 minutes. Be sure mixture does not boil over.
2. Remove the mixture from the heat and let it cool for 5 minutes.
3. Add vodka and vanilla. Stir.

4. Store in any empty 750-ml. liquor bottle with a screw top or another bottle with a resealable lid.

• MAKES 750 ML.

TIDBITS

It is very important that you use a covered saucepan when making this drink. The alcohol will boil away if the solution is not covered when it gets hot.

Also, the longer this drink is bottled and stored in a dark, cool place, the better it will taste. For the best flavor, store it for at least thirty days before drinking. Probably the hardest part of making this simple recipe is not drinking the stuff before it matures!

• • • •

KEEBLER SOFT BATCH CHOCOLATE CHIP COOKIES

☆　　♥　　☎　　✎　　✉　　✂　　☞

In pre–Civil War Philadelphia, Godfrey Keebler earned a reputation for baking the best cookies and crackers around. Keebler joined in a federation with sixteen local and regional bakeries to help form the United Biscuit Company in 1927. This system lasted for twenty-two years, until 1949, when the conglomerate chose to operate under a single name. *Keebler* was judged to be the most sound and memorable. In 1983 Keebler expanded its distribution to the West Coast, making the conglomerate a national concern.

Today Keebler manufactures more than 200 different products from its 83,000-square-foot facility in Elmhurst, Illinois. Those products, including the chewy Soft Batch cookie, are sold in some 75,000 retail outlets nationwide. Total annual sales for the company are in excess of $1.5 billion, making Keebler the second-largest cookie and cracker manufacturer in the United States, with popular products that have been enjoyed by five generations of Americans.

1 pound (4 sticks) butter,
　　softened
2 eggs
2 tablespoons molasses
2 teaspoons vanilla extract
⅓ cup water
1½ cups granulated sugar

1½ cups packed brown sugar
1 teaspoon baking powder
1½ teaspoons baking soda
1 teaspoon salt
5 cups all-purpose flour
1½ twelve-ounce packages
　　semisweet chocolate chips

1. Preheat the oven to 375°F.
2. Cream the butter, eggs, molasses, vanilla, and water in a medium-size bowl.

3. In a large bowl, sift together the sugars, baking powder, baking soda, salt, and flour.
4. Combine the moist mixture with the dry mixture. Add the chocolate chips.
5. Shape the dough into 1-inch balls, and place them 1 inch apart on an ungreased cookie sheet.
6. Bake for 8 minutes, or until light brown around edges.

• MAKES 4 DOZEN COOKIES

Pepperidge Farm® Chesapeake® and Sausalito® Cookies
Pepperidge Farm products bear the name of the farm where Margaret Rudkin lived and created her first product. It was on that farm in Fairfield, Connecticut, in 1937 that Mrs. Rudkin baked her first loaf of homemade bread for her children. Her first few loaves turned out terribly, but she was persistent and eventually came up with a loaf of bread so delicious that friends began requesting it. Soon Mrs. Rudkin was baking as a commercial venture and adding new products. In 1961 Pepperidge Farm was purchased by the Campbell Soup Company. Six years later Margaret Rudkin passed away at the age of sixty-nine.

But Mrs. Rudkin's kitchen enterprise lives on and is bigger than ever. Today Pepperidge Farm has more than 300 products in distribution. One of them is the crispy Chesapeake cookie.

Simply follow the recipe for the Keebler Soft Batch cookie with these exceptions: Omit the water and molasses. Add 3 cups of chopped pecans. (For the Sausalito cookie, substitute macadamia nuts.) Bake at the same temperature, but for 10 to 11 minutes rather than 8 minutes. This will make the cookies crispier.

•   •   •   •

KFC
BUTTERMILK
BISCUITS

☆　♥　☎　✎　✉　✂　☛

In 1991 Kentucky Fried Chicken bigwigs decided to improve the image of America's third-largest fast-food chain. As a more health-conscious society began to affect sales of fried chicken, the company changed its name to KFC and introduced a lighter fare of skinless chicken. The company is now working hard on developing a new line of baked and roasted chicken.

In the last forty years KFC has experienced extraordinary growth. Five years after first franchising the business, Colonel Harland Sanders had 400 outlets in the United States and Canada. Four years later there were more than 600 franchises, including one in England, the first overseas outlet. In 1964 John Y. Brown, Jr., twenty-nine, a young Louisville lawyer, and Jack Massey, sixty, a Nashville financier, bought the Colonel's business for $2 million. Only seven years later, in 1971, Heublein, Inc., bought the KFC Corporation for $275 million. Then in 1986, for a whopping $840 million, PepsiCo added KFC to its conglomerate, which now includes Pizza Hut and Taco Bell. That means PepsiCo owns more fast-food outlets than any other company including McDonald's—totaling over 20,000.

At each KFC restaurant, workers blend real buttermilk with a flour mixture to create the well-known buttermilk biscuits that have been a popular menu item since their introduction in 1982.

½ cup (1 stick) butter
2½ tablespoons granulated sugar
1 beaten egg
¾ cup buttermilk

¼ cup club soda
1 teaspoon salt
5 cups Bisquick biscuit mix

1. Preheat the oven to 450°F.
2. Combine all of the ingredients. Knead the dough by hand until smooth.
3. Flour your hands. Pat the dough flat to ¾-inch thickness on waxed paper and punch out biscuits with a biscuit cutter.
4. Bake on a greased baking sheet for 12 minutes, or until golden brown.

- MAKES 18 BISCUITS

TIDBITS

To produce biscuits that most closely resemble the KFC variety, it is best to use a biscuit cutter for this recipe, as specified above. If you don't have a biscuit cutter, the lid of an aerosol can will suffice—just be sure it's not from a product that is toxic. A lid from a can of nonstick cooking spray, for example, works great.

If all you have is a lid from a can of Raid bug spray, I would say that you should form the biscuits as best you can with your bare hands.

• • • •

KFC
COLE SLAW

☆ ♥ ☎ ✎ ✉ ✄ ☞

In 1935, shortly after the first Kentucky Fried Chicken restaurant had opened, Governor Ruby Laffoon made Harland Sanders a Kentucky colonel in recognition of his contribution to the state's cuisine. In 1952, at the age of sixty-six, Colonel Sanders began to franchise his fried chicken business. Traveling through Ohio, Indiana, and Kentucky, he met with restaurant owners, cooking his chicken for them and their employees. If the restaurant owners liked the chicken, they would agree with a handshake that the Colonel would supply the "secret blend" of spices in exchange for a nickel on each piece of chicken sold. As of 1991 there were more than 8,000 Kentucky Fried Chicken stores worldwide, with sales of more than $5 billion.

The recipe for the Colonel's cole slaw, which is made from scratch in each store, is kept as secret as that for the herbs and spices in the fried chicken. Now taste our "top-secret" version of the Colonel's well-known favorite slaw.

8 cups very finely chopped
   cabbage (1 head)
1/4 cup shredded carrot
   (1 medium carrot)
1/3 cup granulated sugar
1/2 teaspoon salt

1/8 teaspoon pepper
1/4 cup milk
1/2 cup mayonnaise
1/4 cup buttermilk
1 1/2 tablespoons white vinegar
2 1/2 tablespoons lemon juice

1. Be sure that the cabbage and carrots are chopped up into very fine pieces (about the size of rice kernels).
2. Combine the sugar, salt, pepper, milk, mayonnaise, buttermilk, vinegar, and lemon juice, and beat until smooth.

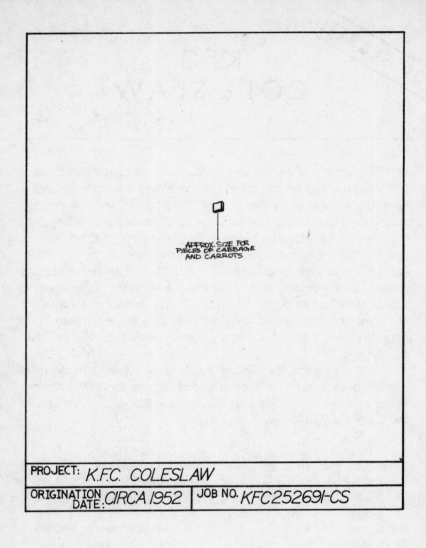

APPROX. SIZE FOR
PIECES OF CABBAGE
AND CARROTS

PROJECT: *K.F.C. COLESLAW*	
ORIGINATION DATE: *CIRCA 1952*	JOB NO. *KFC252691-CS*

3. Add the cabbage and carrots. Mix well.
4. Cover and refrigerate for at least 2 hours before serving.

• SERVES 8

TIDBITS

The critical part of this cole slaw recipe is the flavor-enhancement period prior to eating. Be absolutely certain the cole slaw sits in the refrigerator for at least a couple of hours prior to serving for a great-tasting slew of slaw.

•   •   •   •

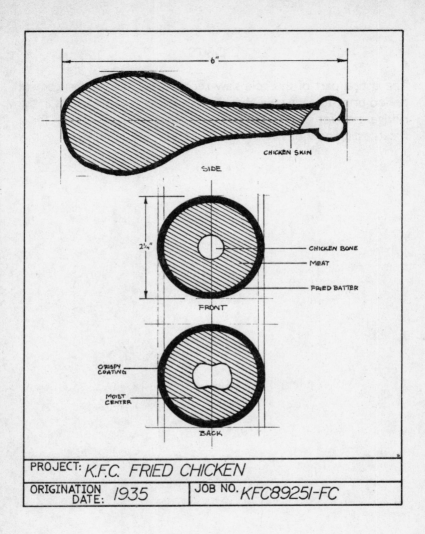

6"

CHICKEN SKIN

SIDE

2¼"

CHICKEN BONE

MEAT

FRIED BATTER

FRONT

CRISPY COATING

MOIST CENTER

BACK

PROJECT: *K.F.C. FRIED CHICKEN*

ORIGINATION DATE: *1935*

JOB NO. *KFC89251-FC*

KFC
ORIGINAL RECIPE
FRIED CHICKEN

☆　　♥　　☎　　✎　　✉　　✂　　☛

Since 1952, when Colonel Harland Sanders opened his first franchise, only a select few have been privy to the secret "herbs and spices" contained in the billion-dollar blend. To protect the top-secret recipe, the company claims, portions of the secret blend are premixed at two confidential spice companies and then distributed to KFC's offices, where they are combined. In 1983, in his book *Big Secrets*, author William Poundstone hired a laboratory to analyze a dry sampling of the spice mixture. The surprising discovery was that instead of identifying "eleven herbs and spices," the analysis showed only four ingredients: flour, salt, pepper, and monosodium glutamate, a flavor enhancer.

The cooking procedure is believed to be the other half of the secret. Colonel Sanders became famous for using a pressure cooker shortly after its invention in 1939. He discovered that hungry travelers greatly appreciated the ten-minute pressure-cooking process (compared to the half hour it used to take for frying chicken), and the new process made the chicken juicy and moist inside.

KFC is the third-largest fast-food chain in the country, and uses around 500 million chickens every year.

6 cups Crisco cooking oil
1 egg, beaten
2 cups milk
2 cups all-purpose flour
4 tablespoons salt
2 teaspoons black pepper

1 teaspoon MSG (monosodium glutamate—you can use Accent Flavor Enhancer)
2 frying chickens with skin, each cut into 8 pieces

1. Pour the oil into the pressure cooker and heat over medium heat to about 400°F.
2. In a small bowl, combine the egg and milk.
3. In a separate bowl, combine the remaining four dry ingredients.
4. Dip each piece of chicken into the milk until fully moistened.
5. Roll the moistened chicken in the flour mixture until completely coated.
6. In groups of four or five, drop the covered chicken pieces into the oil and lock the lid in place.
7. When steam begins shooting through the pressure release, set the timer for 10 minutes.
8. After 10 minutes, release the pressure according to manufacturer's instructions, and remove the chicken to paper towels or a metal rack to drain. Repeat with the remaining chicken.

• MAKES 12 PIECES

TIDBITS

If you prefer not to use MSG, you may substitute an additional ½ tablespoon of salt. Be aware, however, that using MSG produces the best clone of KFC's Fried Chicken.

•   •   •   •

LONG JOHN SILVER'S BATTER-DIPPED FISH

☆ ♥ ☎ ✎ ✉ ✂ ☞

Jerrico, Inc., the parent company for Long John Silver's Seafood Shoppes, got its start in 1929 as a six-stool hamburger stand called the White Tavern Shoppe. Jerrico was started by a man named Jerome Lederer, who watched Long John Silver's thirteen units dwindle in the shadow of World War II to just three units. Then, with determination, he began rebuilding.

In 1946 Jerome launched a new restaurant called Jerry's, and it was a booming success, with growth across the country. Then he took a chance on what would be his most successful venture in 1969, with the opening of the first Long John Silver's Fish 'n' Chips. The name was inspired by Robert Louis Stevenson's *Treasure Island.*

In 1991 there were 1,450 Long John Silver Seafood Shoppes in thirty-seven states, Canada, and Singapore, with annual sales of more than $781 million. That means the company holds about 65 percent of the $1.2-billion quick-service seafood business.

3 cups soybean oil
2 pounds fresh cod fillets
1⅓ cups self-rising flour
1 cup water

1 egg
2 teaspoons granulated sugar
2 teaspoons salt

1. Heat the oil in a deep pan to about 400°F.
2. Cut the fish into approximately 7 × 2-inch wedges.
3. With a mixer, blend the flour, water, egg, sugar, and salt.
4. Dip each fillet into the batter, coating generously, and quickly drop into the oil.

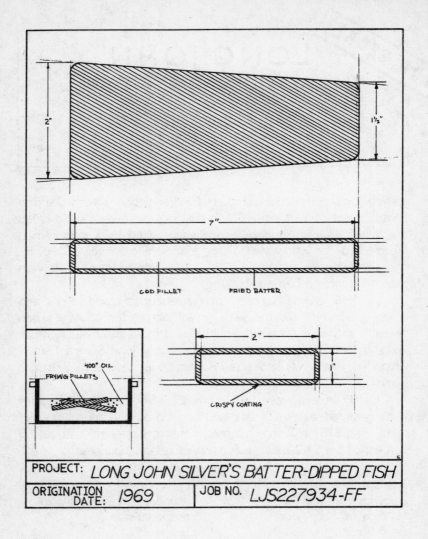

2"

1½"

7"

COD FILLET   FRIED BATTER

400° OIL

FRYING FILLETS

2"

1"

CRISPY COATING

PROJECT: *LONG JOHN SILVER'S BATTER-DIPPED FISH*

ORIGINATION DATE: *1969*   **JOB NO.** *LJS227934-FF*

5. Fry each fillet until dark golden brown, about 5 minutes.
6. Remove from the oil and place on paper towels or a metal rack to drain.

• MAKES 4 TO 6 FILLETS

TIDBITS

Soybean oil is what your local Long John Silver's uses to fry their fish, and you will best duplicate the real thing by using the same oil. But any other oil may be substituted. You might want to try canola oil. It is the oil lowest in saturated fat, and the taste difference is only slight.

It's crucial that your oil be hot before frying the fish. To test the temperature, drip some batter into the oil. It should bubble rapidly. After 5 minutes, the test batter should become golden brown. If so, fry away, fish fiends.

•   •   •   •

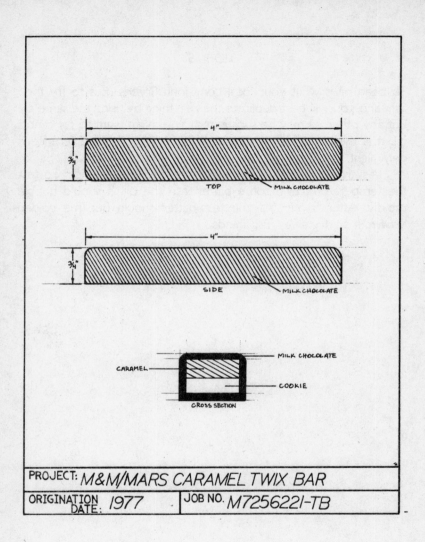

4"

3/4"

TOP

MILK CHOCOLATE

4"

3/4"

SIDE

MILK CHOCOLATE

MILK CHOCOLATE

CARAMEL

COOKIE

CROSS SECTION

PROJECT: M&M/MARS CARAMEL TWIX BAR

ORIGINATION DATE: 1977

JOB NO. M7256221-TB

M&M/MARS
CARAMEL
TWIX BARS

☆　♥　☎　✎　✉　✂　☛

The process by which M&M/Mars and other candy companies smoothly chocolate-coat their confections is called *enrobing*. Enrobing was created in 1900 to protect the interiors from drying out. The process begins when the uncoated centers pass through a curtain of liquid chocolate on a continuous stainless-steel belt. The top and sides of each bar are coated. The process is repeated a second time, and then the fully coated bar is quickly cooled and wrapped.

Enrobing is the least expensive way for manufacturers to coat their chocolates. At M&M/Mars, the enrobing machines run around the clock to meet the high demand for their products. Unfortunately, traditional kitchen appliances don't include among them an enrobing machine, so in our case, dipping will have to suffice.

The caramel Twix was introduced in 1977, and peanut butter Twix came along in 1982. Other variations of the bar, including cookies & cream and fudge, were introduced in the early nineties.

35 unwrapped Kraft caramels
1 box (40) Nabisco Lorna Doone
　shortbread cookies

Two 12-ounce bags milk-
　chocolate chips

1. Combine the caramels with the water in a small pan and melt over low heat.
2. Place the shortbread cookies side by side on an ungreased cookie sheet.
3. Spoon a dab of caramel onto each cookie. Then place all the cookies in the refrigerator until the caramel firms up.

4. In the meantime, in a double boiler over low heat, melt the chocolate chips. You may also use the microwave for melting the chocolate. Just zap the chips for 1 minute on high, stir, then zap 'em for another minute.
5. Remove the cookies from the refrigerator. Rest each one on a fork and dip it into the chocolate. Tap the fork on the side of the pan or bowl to knock off any excess chocolate. Then place each one on a sheet of waxed paper and let them cool at room temperature (65 to 70°F). This could take several hours, but the bars will set best this way. If you want to speed up the process, put the candy in the refrigerator for 30 minutes.

• MAKES 40 BARS

M&M/Mars Peanut Butter Twix® Bars

Substitute 1 cup of peanut butter sweetened with ½ cup powdered sugar for the caramels. The peanut-butter mixture will be of a consistency that allows you to spread it on the shortbread cookies with your fingers. Follow the rest of the directions exactly.

• • • •

M&M/MARS
SNICKERS BAR

☆   ♥   ☎   ✎   ✉   ✄   ☛

In 1992 *Fortune* magazine estimated the Mars family's personal worth at somewhere around $12.5 billion—quite a fistful of peanuts. This solid foundation of wealth, built on the country's undying passion for chocolate and other sweets, has made this clan the richest family in America—and the most reclusive. A family rule prohibits photographs to be taken of the Mars family and corporate executives. According to *Fortune,* a photographer who once tried to get a shot of Forrest Mars, Sr., found himself enveloped in a cloth that was thrown as he was about to snap the picture.

The empire started in 1902, when nineteen-year-old Franklin C. Mars began selling homemade candy. In 1910 he started a wholesale candy business in Tacoma, Washington. Ten years later Frank moved to Minneapolis, where he used the family kitchen to make buttercreams, which were personally delivered to retailers in the city by his wife, Ethel. Business grew steadily, and in 1940 Frank's son Forrest established M&M Limited in Newark, New Jersey.

By 1967 the family's confectionery business in the United States had been consolidated into M&M/Mars. The fortune grew steadily larger as the corporation routinely kept four brands in the top-ten-selling chocolates in the country: Milky Way, M&M's Plain and Peanut, and, in the number-one spot, Snickers.

1 tablespoon plus ¼ cup water	*35 unwrapped Kraft caramels*
¼ cup light corn syrup	*1 cup (or two 3.5-ounce*
2 tablespoons butter	*packages) dry-roasted*
1 teaspoon vanilla extract	*unsalted peanuts*
2 tablespoons peanut butter	*Two 12-ounce bags milk-*
Dash salt	*chocolate chips*
3 cups powdered sugar	

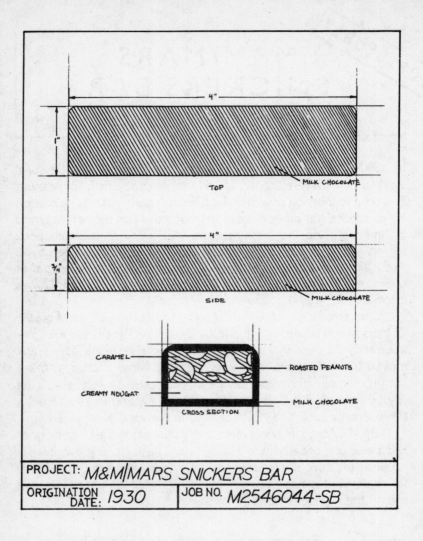

4"

1"

TOP

MILK CHOCOLATE

4"

3/4"

SIDE

MILK CHOCOLATE

CARAMEL

ROASTED PEANUTS

CREAMY NOUGAT

MILK CHOCOLATE

CROSS SECTION

PROJECT: M&M/MARS SNICKERS BAR

ORIGINATION DATE: 1930

JOB NO. M2546044-SB

1. With the mixer on high speed, combine 1 tablespoon water, corn syrup, butter, vanilla, peanut butter, and salt until creamy. Slowly add the powdered sugar.
2. When the mixture has the consistency of dough, remove it from the bowl with your hands and press it into a lightly greased 9 × 9-inch pan. Set in the refrigerator.

3. Melt the caramels in a small pan with ¼ cup water over low heat.
4. When the caramel is soft, mix in the peanuts. Pour the mixture over the refrigerated nougat in the pan. Let this cool in the refrigerator.
5. When the refrigerated mixture is firm, melt the chocolate over low heat in a double boiler or in a microwave oven set on high for 2 minutes. Stir halfway through cooking time.
6. When the mixture in the pan has hardened, cut it into 2 × 1-inch sections.
7. Set each chunk onto a fork and dip into the melted chocolate. Tap the fork against the side of the bowl or pan to knock off any excess chocolate. Then place the chunks on waxed paper to cool at room temperature (less than 70°F). This could take several hours, but the bars will set best this way. You can speed up the process by placing the bars in the refrigerator for 30 minutes.

• MAKES ABOUT 2 DOZEN BARS

• • • •

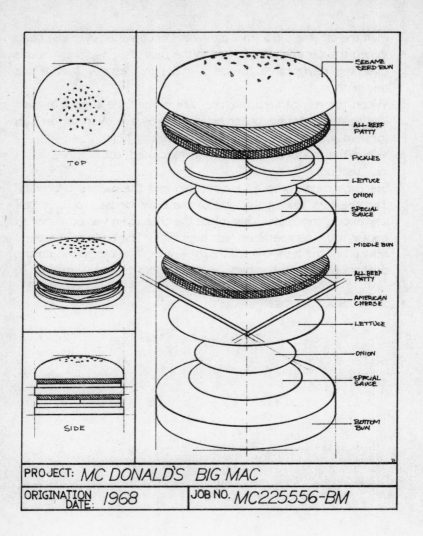

TOP

SIDE

SESAME SEED BUN

ALL-BEEF PATTY

PICKLES

LETTUCE

ONION

SPECIAL SAUCE

MIDDLE BUN

ALL-BEEF PATTY

AMERICAN CHEESE

LETTUCE

ONION

SPECIAL SAUCE

BOTTOM BUN

PROJECT: *MC DONALD'S BIG MAC*

ORIGINATION DATE: *1968*

JOB NO. *MC225556-BM*

80

McDONALD'S
BIG MAC

☆   ♥   ☎   ✎   ✉   ✂   ☞

Brothers Dick and Mac McDonald opened the first McDonald's drive-in restaurant in 1948, in San Bernardino, California. When the brothers began to order an increasing amount of restaurant equipment for their growing business, they aroused the curiosity of milkshake machine–salesman Ray Kroc. Kroc befriended the brothers and became a franchising agent for the company that same year, opening his first McDonald's in Des Plaines, Illinois. Kroc later founded the hugely successful McDonald's Corporation and perfected the fast-food system that came to be studied and duplicated by other chains over the years.

The first day Kroc's cash register rang up $366.12. Today the company racks up about $50 million a day in sales in more than 12,000 outlets worldwide, and for the past ten years a new store has opened somewhere around the world an average of every fifteen hours.

The double-decker Big Mac was introduced in 1968, the brainchild of a local franchisee. It is now the world's most popular hamburger.

1 sesame-seed hamburger bun
Half of an additional hamburger
    bun
¼ pound ground beef
Dash salt
1 tablespoon Kraft Thousand
    Island dressing

1 teaspoon finely diced onion
½ cup chopped lettuce
1 slice American cheese
2 to 3 dill pickle slices

1. With a serrated knife, cut the top off the extra bun half, leaving about a ¾-inch-thick slice. This will be the middle bun in your sandwich.

2. Place the three bun halves on a hot pan or griddle, face down, and toast them to a light brown. Set aside, but keep the pan hot.
3. Divide the ground beef in half and press into two thin patties slightly larger than bun.
4. Cook the patties in the hot pan over medium heat for 2 to 3 minutes on each side. Salt lightly.
5. Build the burger in the following stacking order from the bottom up:

bottom bun	remainder of dressing
half of dressing	remainder of onion
half of onion	remainder of lettuce
half of lettuce	pickle slices
American cheese	beef patty
beef patty	top bun
middle bun	

• MAKES 1 HAMBURGER

TIDBITS

To build a Big Mac Jr.® (it is sold on a "limited time only" basis), follow this stacking order from the bottom up:

bottom bun	½ teaspoon finely diced onion
beef patty	½ tablespoon Kraft
American cheese slice	Thousand Island dressing
2 pickle slices	top bun
¼ cup chopped lettuce	

Using real American cheese slices, not processed cheese food, will yield the best "taste-alike" results. Since the beef patties must be very thin, you may find it easier to cook them slightly frozen (like the real thing).

McDONALD'S EGG McMUFFIN

☆   ♥   ☎   ✎   ✉   ✂   ☛

In March 1988 the first McDonald's in Belgrade, Yugoslavia, set an all-time opening-day record by running 6,000 people under the arches. And in early 1990, when a Moscow McDonald's opened, it became the busiest in the world by serving more than 20,000 people in just the first month of operation. The McDonald's Rome franchise racks up annual sales of more than $11 million. And in August of 1992, the world's largest McDonald's opened in China. The Beijing McDonald's seats 700 people in 28,000 square feet. It has over 1,000 employees, and parking for 200 employee bicycles. McDonald's outlets dot the globe in fifty-two countries today, including Turkey, Thailand, Panama, El Salvador, Indonesia, and Poland. In fact, about 40 percent of the McDonald's that open today stand on foreign soil—that's more than 3,000 outlets.

Back in the United States, McDonald's serves one of every four breakfasts eaten out of the home. The Egg McMuffin sandwich was introduced in 1977 and has become a convenient breakfast-in-a-sandwich for millions. The name for the sandwich was not the brainstorm of a corporate think tank as you would expect, but rather a suggestion from ex-McDonald's chairman and CEO Fred Turner. He says his wife Patty came up with it.

You will need an empty clean can with the same diameter as an English muffin. (A 6½-ounce tuna can works best.)

1 English muffin	1 egg
1 slice Canadian bacon	1 slice American cheese

1. Split the English muffin and brown each face in a hot pan. Set aside. Keep the pan on medium heat.

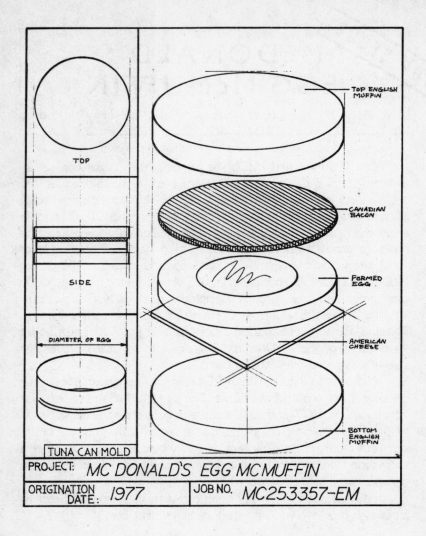

TOP

SIDE

DIAMETER OF EGG

TUNA CAN MOLD

TOP ENGLISH MUFFIN

CANADIAN BACON

FORMED EGG

AMERICAN CHEESE

BOTTOM ENGLISH MUFFIN

PROJECT: *MC DONALD'S EGG MC MUFFIN*

ORIGINATION DATE: *1977*

JOB NO. *MC253357-EM*

2. In a frying pan of boiling water, cook the Canadian bacon for 10 minutes.
3. Grease the inside of the can with shortening or coat with a nonstick spray.
4. Place the greased can in the hot pan over medium heat and crack the egg into the center.

5. Break the yolk. Lightly salt the egg.
6. When the surface of the egg begins to firm, cut around the inside of the can with a butter knife to free the edges.
7. Pull the can off the egg; turn the egg over and cook for 1 minute more.
8. Build the sandwich in the following stacking order from the bottom up:

bottom English muffin	Canadian bacon
American cheese	top English muffin
egg	

9. Microwave for 15 to 20 seconds on high for uniform heating, if desired.

• MAKES 1 SANDWICH

TIDBITS

For a closer clone, use real American cheese slices, not processed cheese food.

•   •   •   •

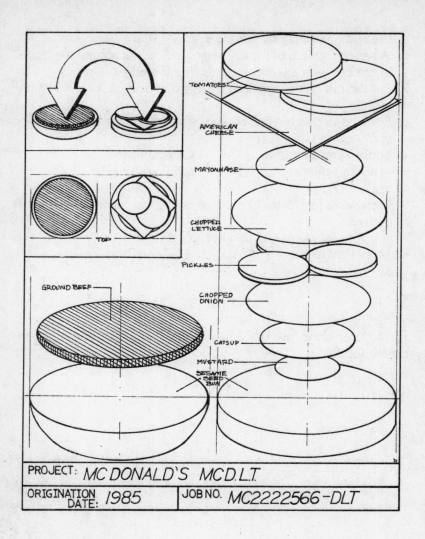

TOMATOES

AMERICAN CHEESE

MAYONNAISE

CHOPPED LETTUCE

PICKLES

CHOPPED ONION

CATSUP

MUSTARD

SESAME SEED BUN

GROUND BEEF

TOP

PROJECT:	*MC DONALD'S MCD.L.T.*	
ORIGINATION DATE: *1985*	JOB NO.	*MC2222566-DLT*

86

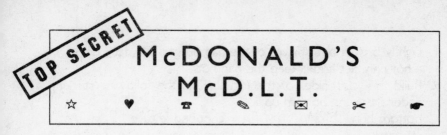

McDONALD'S
McD.L.T.

☆   ♥   ☎   ✎   ✉   ✂   ☞

And how about this . . . ?

In 1963 the busiest clown in America, Ronald McDonald, made his debut in Washington, D.C. But beneath that red wig and 14½-inch shoes was someone who would later become the portly weatherman on NBC's "Today" show. You got it, Willard Scott.

Future Ronald McDonald wanna-bes get their training at McDonald's so-called college, just as many of the chain's managers and franchise owners do. It is a surprisingly busy institution. By 1991 the 40,000th student was granted a Hamburgerology Degree from McDonald's Hamburger University in Oak Brook, Illinois. (Hamburger University was set up to provide instruction for McDonald's personnel in the various aspects of their business—equipment, controls, human relations skills, and management skills.)

Nearly 3,000 students pass through the halls of the school each year as they continue to grow in their McDonald's careers. And the American Council on Education has approved eighteen of the university's courses for college credit.

One more chapter in the studies of H.U. graduates came in 1985, when the "hot side" and "cool side" of the McD.L.T. found their way onto McDonald's menu. It lives on only in this book, for five years after it was introduced, the McD.L.T. was dropped and replaced with the McLean Deluxe.

1 sesame-seed hamburger bun
⅛ teaspoon prepared mustard
1 teaspoon catsup
2 medium onion rings, chopped
3 dill pickle slices
¼ cup chopped lettuce

1 tablespoon mayonnaise
1 slice American cheese
2 tomato slices
¼ pound ground beef
Dash salt

1. Lightly brown both halves of the hamburger bun, face down, in a hot pan. Set aside; keep the pan hot.
2. Build the "cool side" of the McD.L.T. in the following stacking order from the bottom up:

bottom bun	chopped lettuce
mustard	mayonnaise
catsup	American cheese slice
chopped onion	tomato slices
pickle slices	

3. With your hands, form the ground beef into a thin patty slightly larger in diameter than the bun.
4. Cook the patty in the hot pan for 2 to 3 minutes per side. Salt lightly.
5. Build the "hot side" in the following stacking order from the bottom up:
   top bun
   beef patty
6. When you are ready to eat, slap the "cool side" and the "hot side" together.

• MAKES I HAMBURGER

•   •   •   •

MRS. FIELDS CHOCOLATE CHIP COOKIES

☆　♥　☎　✎　✉　✂　☞

In 1975 eighteen-year-old Debbi Sivyer perfected the chocolate chip cookies she had been making since the age of twelve. Little did she know then that her delicious cookies would soon launch her into a successful career with her own multi-million-dollar business. It happened two years later, when her new husband, financial consultant Randy Fields, noticed that his clients couldn't resist the batches of cookies that Debbi sent to work with him. With the help of Randy and a banker who lent her $50,000 because he loved her chocolate chip cookies so much, she opened her first cookie store in Palo Alto, California, in 1977. The second store opened two years later in San Francisco.

Without spending a dollar on advertising, the Mrs. Fields Company is now listed on the London Stock Exchange, claims more than 600 stores worldwide, and has purchased the 113-unit bakery chain, La Petite Boulangerie, from PepsiCo.

1 cup (2 sticks) softened butter
½ cup granulated sugar
1½ cups packed brown sugar
2 eggs
2½ teaspoons vanilla extract
2½ cups all-purpose flour

¾ teaspoon salt
1 teaspoon baking powder
1 teaspoon baking soda
1½ twelve-ounce bags semisweet
    chocolate chips

1. Preheat the oven to 350°F.
2. In a large mixing bowl, cream the butter, sugars, eggs, and vanilla.
3. Sift together the flour, salt, baking powder, and baking soda.
4. Combine the wet and dry ingredients.

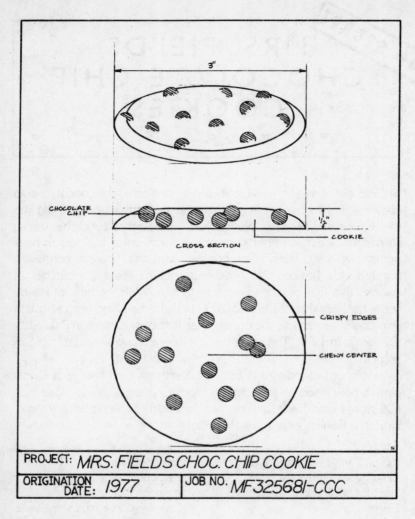

3"

CHOCOLATE CHIP

CROSS SECTION

1½"

COOKIE

CRISPY EDGES

CHEWY CENTER

PROJECT: *MRS. FIELDS CHOC. CHIP COOKIE*

ORIGINATION DATE: *1977*

JOB NO. *MF325681-CCC*

5. Stir in the chocolate chips.
6. With your fingers, place golf-ball-size dough portions 2 inches apart on an ungreased cookie sheet.
7. Bake for 9 minutes, or until edges are light brown.

• MAKES 30 COOKIES

TIDBITS

It's very important that you not exceed the cooking time given above, even if the cookies appear to be underbaked. When the cookies are removed from the oven, the sugar in them will stay hot and continue the cooking process. The finished product should be soft in the middle and crunchy around the edges.

For variations of this cookie, substitute milk chocolate for the semisweet chocolate and/or add 1½ cups of chopped walnuts or macadamia nuts to the recipe before baking. Although you can substitute margarine for butter in this recipe, you will have the best results from butter. The cookie will have a richer taste and will be crispier around the edges like the original.

●　　●　　●　　●

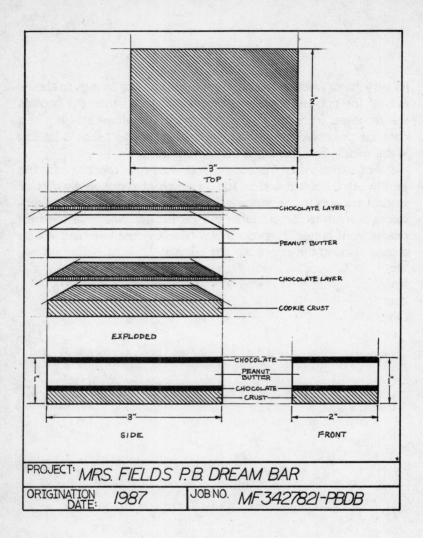

TOP

CHOCOLATE LAYER

PEANUT BUTTER

CHOCOLATE LAYER

COOKIE CRUST

EXPLODED

CHOCOLATE
PEANUT
BUTTER
CHOCOLATE
CRUST

SIDE

FRONT

PROJECT: MRS. FIELDS P.B. DREAM BAR

ORIGINATION DATE: 1987

JOB NO. MF342782I-PBDB

MRS. FIELDS PEANUT BUTTER DREAM BARS

☆   ♥   ☎   ✎   ✉   ✂   ☛

In 1987 the Mrs. Fields Corporation devised a rather clever treat called the Peanut Butter Dream Bar—a delicious combination of peanut butter, chocolate, and a cookie-crumb crust. It was not only a tasty product but an economical one. Mrs. Fields has always had the policy of removing cookies that are more than two hours old from outlet display cases. Now, instead of being thrown away, the cookies are crumbled up and mixed with melted butter to form the Dream Bar crust.

8 Mrs. Fields Chocolate Chip
    Cookies (see previous
    recipe)
5 tablespoons melted butter

¾ cup peanut butter
1½ cups powdered sugar
One 12-ounce bag milk-chocolate
    chips

1. Preheat the oven to 350°F.
2. Crumble the cookies into a medium mixing bowl.
3. Add the melted butter; stir until the mixture darkens and the butter is evenly mixed in.
4. Pour the mixture into an ungreased 9 × 9-inch baking pan.
5. Press the dough down solidly into the pan and bake for 10 minutes, or until firm around edges. When done, cool in the refrigerator.
6. Mix the peanut butter and sugar until blended. The mixture should have a doughy texture that allows you to knead it with your hands.
7. Melt the chocolate chips in a double boiler over low heat, stirring

often. You may also melt them in a microwave oven set on high for 2 minutes, stirring halfway through the heating time.

8. When the dough is cool, spread half of the melted chocolate over the surface.
9. Cool in the refrigerator for 20 to 30 minutes, or until hardened.
10. Spread the peanut butter mixture evenly over the surface of the chocolate.
11. Spread the remaining chocolate over the peanut butter, covering to the edges of the pan.
12. Cool the finished product in the refrigerator or let it sit at room temperature until hardened.
13. Slice into five even rows and then once down the middle.

• MAKES 10 BARS

• • • •

ORANGE JULIUS

☆ ♥ ☎ ✎ ✉ ✂ ☞

In 1926 a man named Julius Freed opened a fresh-orange-juice shop in downtown Los Angeles, initially ringing up sales of $20 a day. The real estate agent who helped locate his first store just so happened to be an ex-chemist named Bill Hamlin. The two became good friends. One day Hamlin, drawing on his chemistry background, presented Freed with an idea for a compound, using all natural ingredients, that would give his orange juice a creamy, frothy texture. When the two began selling the new drink, response was so tremendous that sales skyrocketed to $100 a day. An increasing number of customers would come by the store saying, "Give me an orange, Julius," and so the name was born. By 1929 the chain had opened 100 stores across the United States.

In 1987 International Dairy Queen bought the Orange Julius chain, and today you'll find more than 500 Orange Julius outlets nationwide serving the drink in a variety of natural flavors, including strawberry and pineapple.

1 cup orange juice	¾ teaspoon vanilla extract
1 cup water	¼ cup granulated sugar
2 egg whites	1 heaping cup ice

Combine all of the ingredients in a blender set on high speed for 15–30 seconds.

• MAKES 2 DRINKS

• • • •

PANCAKES FROM INTERNATIONAL HOUSE OF PANCAKES

☆   ♥   ☎   ✎   ✉   ✂   ☞

Al Lupin opened the first International House of Pancakes in Toluca Lake, California, in 1958. Now, more than thirty years later, the company has added 490 restaurants, which together serve more than 400,000 pancakes on an average day. That's enough pancakes to make a stack 8,000 feet tall! For comparison, the huge stack of flapjacks would dwarf Chicago's Sears Tower, the world's tallest building, which rises a mere 1,454 feet.

Nonstick spray
1¼ cups all-purpose flour
1 egg
1½ cups buttermilk
¼ cup granulated sugar

1 heaping teaspoon baking
   powder
1 teaspoon baking soda
¼ cup cooking oil
¼ teaspoon salt

1. Preheat a skillet over medium heat. Use a pan with a nonstick surface or apply a little nonstick spray.
2. In a blender or with a mixer, combine all of the remaining ingredients until smooth.

3. Pour the batter by spoonfuls into the hot pan, forming 5-inch circles.
4. When the edges appear to harden, flip the pancakes. They should be light brown.
5. Cook on the other side for same amount of time, until light brown.

- MAKES 8 TO 10 PANCAKES

• • • •

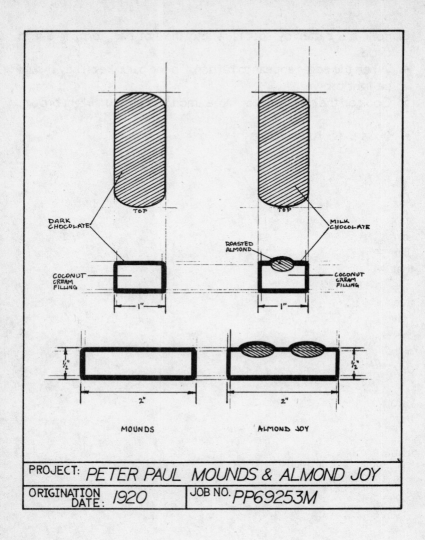

DARK
CHOCOLATE

MILK
CHOCOLATE

ROASTED
ALMOND

TOP

TOP

COCONUT
CREAM
FILLING

COCONUT
CREAM
FILLING

1"

1"

1/2"

1/2"

2"

2"

MOUNDS

ALMOND JOY

PROJECT: *PETER PAUL MOUNDS & ALMOND JOY*

ORIGINATION
DATE: *1920*

JOB NO. *PP69253M*

PETER PAUL MOUNDS AND ALMOND JOY

☆　♥　☎　✎　✉　✂　☛

At the train station in Naugatuck, Connecticut, candy and ice-cream shop owner Peter Paul Halajian used to meet the commuter trains carrying baskets full of fresh hand-made chocolates. The most popular of his candies was a blend of coconut, fruits, nuts, and chocolate that he called *Konabar*.

In 1919, when demand for his confections grew, Halajian and five associates, all of Armenian heritage, opened a business in New Haven to produce and sell his chocolates on a larger scale. Because there were no refrigerators, they made the chocolate by hand at night, when the air was the coolest, and sold the candy during the day. In 1920 the first Mounds bar was introduced.

Peter Paul merged with Cadbury U.S.A. in 1978, and in 1986 Cadbury U.S.A. merged with the Hershey Foods Corporation, now the world's largest candy conglomerate.

Today the recipes for Mounds and Almond Joy are the same as they were in the roaring twenties.

5 ounces Eagle sweetened
    condensed milk
1 teaspoon vanilla extract
2 cups powdered sugar

14 ounces premium shredded or
    flaked coconut
One 24-ounce package semisweet
    chocolate chips

1. Blend the condensed milk and vanilla.
2. Add the powdered sugar to the above mixture a little bit at a time, stirring until smooth.
3. Stir in the coconut. The mixture should be firm.

4. Pat the mixture firmly into a greased 9 × 13 × 2-inch pan. Chill in the refrigerator until firm.
5. In a double boiler over hot (not boiling) water, melt the chocolate, stirring often. You may also use a microwave oven. Place the chips in a bowl and heat for 1 minute on high; stir, then heat for 1 minute more.
6. Remove the coconut mixture from the refrigerator and cut it into 1 × 2-inch bars.
7. Set each coconut bar onto a fork and dip into the chocolate. Tap the fork against the side of the pan or bowl to remove any excess chocolate.
8. Air-dry at room temperature on waxed paper. This could take several hours, but chocolate sets best at cool room temperature (below 70°F). You may speed up the process by placing the bars in the refrigerator for about 30 minutes.

• MAKES ABOUT 3 DOZEN BARS

Peter Paul
Almond Joy
And if you feel like a nut, follow the above recipe with these changes:

1. Add 1 cup dry-roasted almonds to the list of ingredients.
2. Substitute milk-chocolate chips for semisweet chocolate.
3. In step 8, place two almonds atop each bar before dipping.

• • • •

POGEN'S GINGERSNAPS

☆   ♥   ☎   ✎   ✉   ✂   ☛

Back in the 1870s, in the coastal city of Malmö, Sweden, a man named Anders Pahlsson baked the first of his soon-to-be famous gingersnaps in a bakery he named Pogen's. In 1970 Pogen's, Inc., opened in the United States, expanding the line of baked goods that Pahlsson developed in the nineteenth century.

A legend that dates back many years says that if you place a gingersnap in the palm of your hand, press down in the middle, and it breaks into three pieces, good luck will follow. Today, more than 100 years later, good luck and hard work have made Pogen's the third-largest supplier of cookies to the growing vending business.

¼ cup (½ stick) butter
½ cup vegetable shortening
1 cup packed brown sugar
¼ cup molasses
1 egg
2¼ cups sifted all-purpose flour

2 teaspoons baking soda
½ teaspoon salt
1 teaspoon powdered ginger
2 teaspoons ground cinnamon
½ teaspoon ground cloves

1. Preheat the oven to 350°F.
2. Cream the butter, shortening, brown sugar, molasses, and egg until light and fluffy.
3. Sift together the dry ingredients; combine both mixtures.
4. Form the dough into walnut-size balls. With floured fingers, press the balls into flat circles on an ungreased cookie sheet.
5. Bake for 8 minutes, or until golden brown.
6. Remove the gingersnaps from the cookie sheet as soon as they are cool and seal in a covered container to preserve their crunch.

• MAKES 4 DOZEN

TIDBITS

If you follow the above recipe, you will be making gingersnaps in a simple circular form. However, Pogen's gingersnaps are made in a smattering of animal shapes. If you would like a more accurate clone of the Pogen's variety, simply sprinkle the dough with flour and roll it flat. Then use animal-shaped cookie cutters to form the dough before baking.

• • • • •

REESE'S PEANUT BUTTER CUPS

☆　♥　☎　✎　✉　✄　☞

In south central Pennsylvania, in 1917, a thirty-eight-year-old man named H. B. Reese moved to Hershey, Pennsylvania, to operate one of Milton Hershey's dairy farms. Inspired by Hershey's success, and possibly urged on by his growing family (he was to have six sons and seven daughters), Reese soon left the dairy to make his living in the candy business. Then in 1923, after achieving a small success with a few products, Reese produced a candy consisting of specially processed peanut butter covered with Hershey's milk chocolate. It changed a struggling candy plant into a solid business concern. During World War II conditions prompted Reese to discontinue his other products and focus on the peanut butter cup. He thereby developed something unique in America's food industry—a major company built and thriving on one product.

In 1963 the names Hershey and Reese were linked once again when the Hershey Foods Corporation purchased the successful H. B. Reese Candy Company. Today the Reese's Peanut Butter Cup often tops the list of America's best-selling candies.

You will need a muffin tin with shallow cups.

1 cup peanut butter	One 12-ounce package Hershey's
¼ teaspoon salt	milk-chocolate chips
½ cup powdered sugar	

1. In a small bowl, mix the peanut butter, salt, and powdered sugar until firm.
2. Slowly melt the chocolate chips in a double boiler over hot, not boiling, water. You may also melt them in a microwave oven set

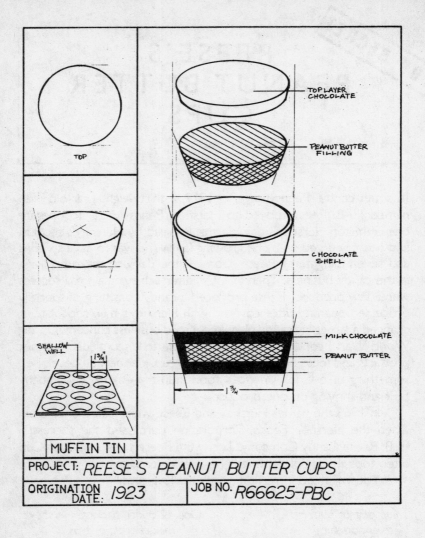

TOP

TOP LAYER
CHOCOLATE

PEANUT BUTTER
FILLING

CHOCOLATE
SHELL

MILK CHOCOLATE

PEANUT BUTTER

$1\frac{3}{4}$

SHALLOW
WELL

$1\frac{3}{4}"$

MUFFIN TIN

PROJECT: *REESE'S PEANUT BUTTER CUPS*

ORIGINATION
DATE: *1923*

JOB NO. *R66625-PBC*

on high for 2 minutes, stirring halfway through the heating time. Add the salt.

3. Grease the muffin-tin cups and spoon some chocolate into each cup, filling halfway.

4. With a spoon, draw the chocolate up the edges of each cup until all sides are coated. Cool in the refrigerator until firm.

5. Spread about a teaspoon of peanut butter onto the chocolate in each cup, leaving room for the final chocolate layer.
6. Pour some chocolate onto the top of each candy and spread it to the edges.
7. Let sit at room temperature, or covered in the refrigerator. Turn out of the pan when firm.

• MAKES 12 PIECES

TIDBITS

It is best to use a shallow muffin tin or candy tin for this recipe. But if you only have the larger, more common, muffin tin, it will work just fine—simply fill each tin only halfway with the chocolate and peanut butter. Unless, that is, you want to make giant-size, mutant peanut butter cups. In that case, fill those cups up all the way!

For even better clones, make your Peanut Butter Cups inside paper baking cups. Cut each baking cup in half horizontally to make it shallower, and "paint" your first layer of chocolate onto the inside of each cup with a spoon. Put the cups into a muffin tin so that they hold their shape, and then put the tin into the refrigerator to set. Add your peanut butter and the top layer of chocolate according to the instructions in the recipe.

•   •   •   •

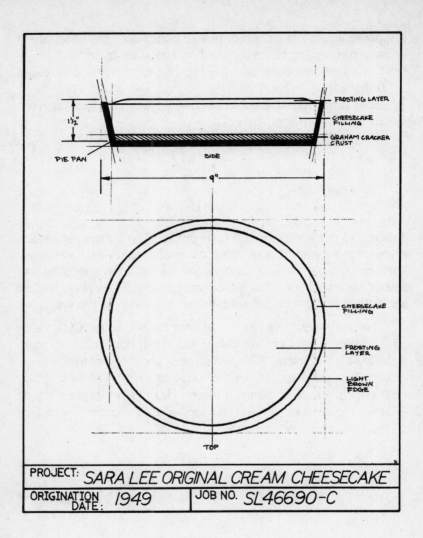

FROSTING LAYER

CHEESECAKE FILLING

GRAHAM CRACKER CRUST

1½"

PIE PAN

SIDE

9"

CHEESECAKE FILLING

FROSTING LAYER

LIGHT BROWN EDGE

TOP

PROJECT: *SARA LEE ORIGINAL CREAM CHEESECAKE*

ORIGINATION DATE: *1949*

JOB NO. *SL46690-C*

SARA LEE ORIGINAL CREAM CHEESECAKE

☆   ♥   ☎   ✎   ✉   ✂   ☛

In 1949 a bakery owner named Charles Lubin pioneered in the frozen-foods business when he invented a top-quality cream cheesecake for sale in supermarkets and restaurants. He named the cheesecake after his daughter, Sara Lee. Though skeptics believed that a frozen bakery item could not be sold in large grocery stores, Lubin's cheesecake was such a success that only two years later, in 1951, he opened the Kitchens of Sara Lee and began to add other items to his line. In the early 1950s Lubin experimented with, and introduced, the aluminum foil pan, which allowed his products to be baked, quickly frozen, and sold in the same container.

Today the Kitchens of Sara Lee produce more than 200 varieties of baked goods. And few people know that this diverse company has also been successful in manufacturing and marketing coffee, meats, and even pantyhose under the Hanes and Liz Claiborne labels.

CRUST
1½ cups fine graham-cracker
   crumbs (11 crackers, rolled)
¼ cup granulated sugar
½ cup (1 stick) butter, softened

FILLING
16 ounces cream cheese
1 cup sour cream
2 tablespoons cornstarch
1 cup granulated sugar
2 tablespoons butter, softened
1 teaspoon vanilla extract

TOPPING
¾ cup sour cream
¼ cup powdered sugar

1. Preheat the oven to 375°F.
2. For the crust, combine the graham-cracker crumbs, sugar, and butter, and mix well.
3. Press the mixture firmly into an ungreased 9-inch pie plate. Press flat onto bottom only.
4. Bake for 8 minutes, or until the edges are slightly brown. Reduce the oven temperature to 350°F.
5. For the filling, combine the cream cheese, sour cream, cornstarch, and sugar in the bowl of a mixer. Mix until the sugar has dissolved.
6. Add the butter and vanilla and blend until smooth. Be careful not to overmix, or the filling will become too fluffy and will crack when cooling.
7. Pour the filling over the crust.
8. Bake for 30 to 35 minutes, or until a knife inserted 1 inch from the edge comes out clean.
9. Cool for 1 hour.
10. For the topping, mix the sour cream and powdered sugar. Spread the mixture over the top of the cooled cheesecake. Chill or freeze until ready to eat.

TIDBITS

If you decide to freeze this cheesecake, defrost it for about an hour at room temperature before serving. You may also defrost slices in the microwave oven if you're in a hurry. (Impatience is a common cheesecake-craving affliction.) Set the microwave on high and zap as follows:

1 slice —15 seconds
2 slices—25 seconds
3 slices—40 seconds

Be sure to refreeze the remaining cheesecake after slicing.

• • • •

SEE'S BUTTERSCOTCH LOLLIPOP

☆ ♥ ☎ ✎ ✉ ✄ ☞

The first See's Candy shop was opened in Los Angeles in 1921 by Charles A. See. He used his mother's candy recipes, and a picture of her at the age of seventy-one embellished every black-and-white box of chocolates. Mary See died in 1939 at the age of eighty-five, but her picture went on to become a symbol of quality and continuity. See's manufacturing plants are still located in California, but because the company will ship anywhere in the United States, it has become a known and respected old-fashioned-style chocolatier across the country.

In an age of automation, many companies that manufacture chocolate have resorted to automated enrobing machines to coat their chocolates. But See's workers still hand-dip much of their candy.

One of the company's most popular sweets isn't dipped at all. It's a hard, rectangular lollipop that comes in chocolate, peanut butter, and butterscotch flavors. The latter, which tastes like caramel, is the most popular flavor of the three, and this recipe will enable you to clone the original, invented more than fifty years ago.

You will need twelve shot glasses, espresso cups, or sake cups for molds, and twelve lollipop sticks or popsicle sticks.

1 cup granulated sugar
1 cup heavy cream
3 tablespoons light corn syrup
2 tablespoons butter or margarine

1 teaspoon vanilla extract
Nonstick spray

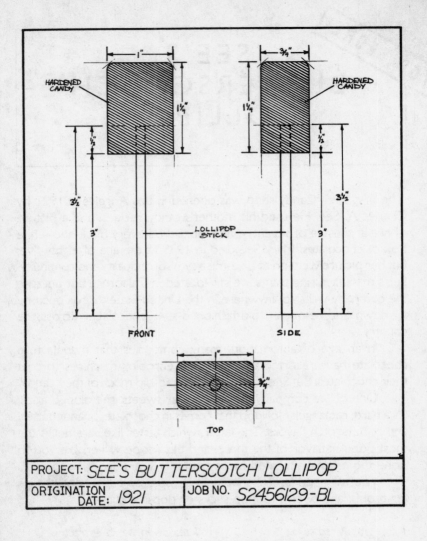

HARDENED CANDY

1"

1¼"

½

3½

3"

FRONT

LOLLIPOP STICK

HARDENED CANDY

3¼"

1¼"

½

3½

3"

SIDE

1"

¾"

TOP

PROJECT: *SEE'S BUTTERSCOTCH LOLLIPOP*

ORIGINATION DATE: *1921*

JOB NO. *S2456129-BL*

1. Combine the first four ingredients in a saucepan over medium heat. Stir until the sugar has dissolved.
2. Let the mixture boil until it reaches 310°F on a cooking thermometer (this is called the *hard-crack stage*), or until a small amount dropped in cold water separates into hard, brittle threads.
3. Stir in the vanilla, then remove from the heat.

4. Coat the molds with nonstick spray and pour the mixture in. (If you are using shot glasses, be sure to cool the mixture first so that the glass won't crack.)
5. Place a small piece of aluminum foil over each mold and press a lollipop stick or popsicle stick in the center.
6. When cool, remove from molds.

• MAKES 1 DOZEN LOLLIPOPS

• • • •

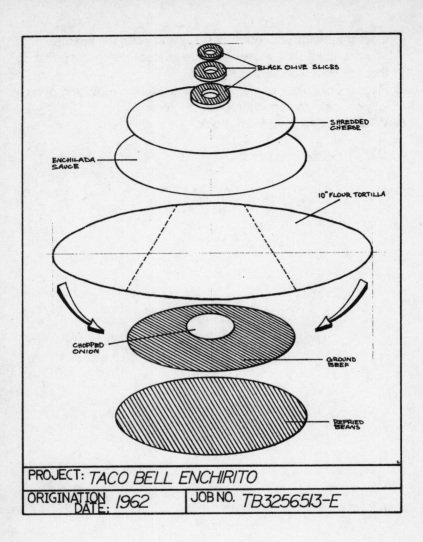

BLACK OLIVE SLICES

SHREDDED
CHEESE

ENCHILADA
SAUCE

10" FLOUR TORTILLA

CHOPPED
ONION

GROUND
BEEF

REFRIED
BEANS

PROJECT: *TACO BELL ENCHIRITO*

ORIGINATION
DATE: *1962*

JOB NO. *TB3256513-E*

TACO BELL ENCHIRITO

An enterprising young man named Glen Bell was fresh out of the Marines in 1946 and was looking for something to do. He worked at a couple of odd jobs, then eventually scraped together $400 in 1947 to buy a hot-dog stand in San Bernardino, California. By 1952 business was so good at Bell's Drive-In that he decided to add hamburgers, just as two brothers named McDonald were starting their own hamburger business in the same city.

Bell soon realized that he needed to expand his menu to differentiate his restaurant from the McDonald brothers'. A fan of Mexican food, Bell devised a way to make tacos and other Mexican specialties quickly and inexpensively. The business grew rapidly, and the name Taco Bell was officially established in 1962, when Bell sold forty company shares to family members at $100 apiece. In 1969, to take his corporation public, he split those original stocks 30,000 to 1.

There are now more than 3,600 Taco Bell units dotting the globe, with total sales in 1991 of $2.8 billion. The company, owned by PepsiCo, Inc., plans to have more than 10,000 outlets by the year 2001.

Today this is the only place you will find the Enchirito. When the product's popularity waned in early 1992, the company said adios.

1 pound ground beef
1/4 teaspoon salt
1 teaspoon chili powder
1/2 tablespoon dried minced onion
One 30-ounce can refried beans
1 package 10- or 12-inch flour
    tortillas

1/4 onion, diced
One 10-ounce can La Victoria
    enchilada sauce
2 1/2 cups shredded cheddar
    cheese
One 2-ounce can sliced black
    olives

1. Slowly brown the ground beef in a skillet, using a wooden spoon or spatula to separate the beef into pea-size pieces.
2. Add the salt, chili powder, and minced onion.
3. With a mixer or a potato masher, beat the refried beans until smooth.
4. Heat the refried beans in a small saucepan or in a microwave oven.
5. Warm the tortillas all at once in a covered container, or wrapped in moist towel in microwave. Set on high for 40 seconds, or warm individually in a skillet over low heat for 2–3 minutes each side.
6. Spoon 3 tablespoons of beef into the center of each tortilla. Sprinkle on ½ teaspoon diced fresh onion. Add ⅓ cup refried beans.
7. Fold the sides of each tortilla over the beans and meat. Flip the tortilla over onto a plate.
8. Spoon 3 tablespoons of enchilada sauce over the top of the tortilla.
9. Sprinkle on ¼ cup shredded cheese.
10. Top with 3 olive slices.

• MAKES 10

•   •   •   •

TASTYKAKE BUTTERSCOTCH KRIMPETS

☆　　♥　　☎　　✎　　✉　　✂　　☞

In 1914 Pittsburgh baker Philip J. Baur and Boston egg salesman Herbert T. Morris decided that there was a need for prewrapped, fresh cakes that were conveniently available at local grocers. The two men coined the name *Tastykake* for their new treats and were determined to use only the finest ingredients, delivered fresh daily to their bakery.

The founders' standards of freshness are still maintained. Tasty-kakes baked tonight are on the shelves tomorrow. That philosophy has contributed to substantial growth for the Tasty Baking Company. On its first day, the firm's sales receipts totaled $28.32; today the company boasts yearly sales of more than $200 million.

Among the top-selling Tastykake treats are the Butterscotch Krimpets, first created in 1927. Today, approximately 6 million Butterscotch Krimpets are baked each and every week.

CAKE
4 egg whites
One 16-ounce box golden pound
*　cake mix*
⅔ cup water

FROSTING
⅛ cup Nestlé Butterscotch Mor-
*　sels (about 40 chips)*
½ (1 stick) cup butter, softened
1½ cups powdered sugar

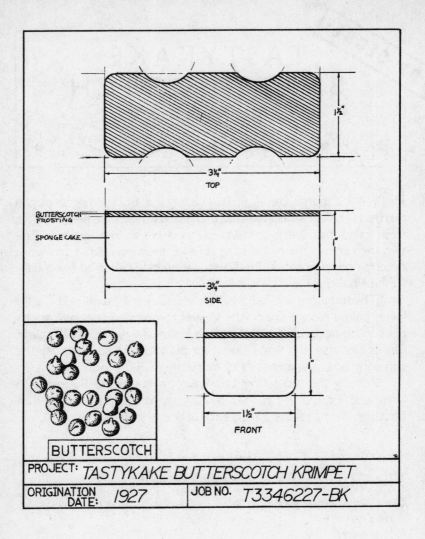

1½"

3¼"

TOP

BUTTERSCOTCH
FROSTING

SPONGE CAKE

1"

3¼"

SIDE

1"

1½"

FRONT

BUTTERSCOTCH

PROJECT: *TASTYKAKE BUTTERSCOTCH KRIMPET*

ORIGINATION
DATE: *1927*

JOB NO. *T3346227-BK*

1. Preheat the oven to 325°F.
2. Beat the egg whites until thick.
3. Blend the egg whites with the cake mix and water.
4. Pour the batter into a greased 9 × 12-inch baking pan. Bake for

30 minutes, or until the top is golden brown and a toothpick inserted in the center comes out clean. Cool.

5. For the frosting, melt the butterscotch morsels in a microwave oven on high for 45 seconds. If you don't have a microwave oven, use a double boiler over hot, not boiling, water.

6. Mix the butter with the melted butterscotch. Add the powdered sugar. Blend with a mixer until the frosting has a smooth consistency.

7. Spread the frosting on top of the cooled pound cake.

8. Cut the cake into nine rows. Then make two cuts lengthwise. This should divide cake into twenty-seven equal pieces.

• MAKES 27 CAKES

•   •   •   •

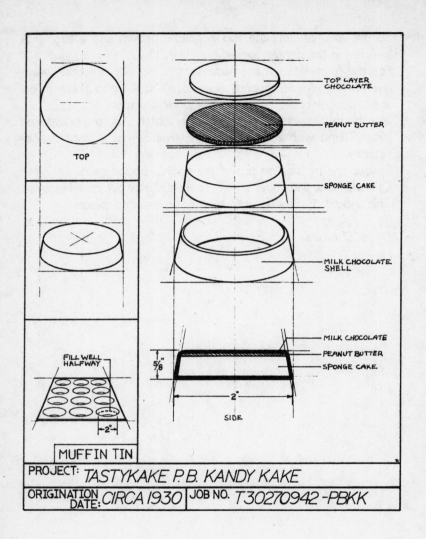

TOP

TOP LAYER CHOCOLATE

PEANUT BUTTER

SPONGE CAKE

MILK CHOCOLATE SHELL

MILK CHOCOLATE
PEANUT BUTTER
SPONGE CAKE

FILL WELL HALFWAY

5/8"

2"

SIDE

2"

MUFFIN TIN

PROJECT: *TASTYKAKE P.B. KANDY KAKE*

ORIGINATION DATE: *CIRCA 1930* JOB NO. *T30270942 –PBKK*

TASTYKAKE PEANUT BUTTER KANDY KAKES

☆　　♥　　☎　　✎　　✉　　✂　　☞

Since it was founded in 1914, the Tasty Baking Company has continued to uphold its policy of controlled distribution to ensure freshness of its products. The company delivers only what it will sell promptly and removes cakes from the stores after just a few days in an effort to keep them from becoming stale.

As the years went by and delivery efficiency improved, transportation routes expanded from Philadelphia to New England, the Midwest, and the South. Mixing, baking, wrapping, and packaging of the products have changed from hand operations to sophisticated automated ones, cutting the production cycle from twelve hours to forty-five minutes, and loading time from five hours to forty-five minutes.

Peanut Butter Kandy Kakes made their debut in the early 1930s as *Tandy Takes*. The name was eventually changed, and the company claims you could make almost 8 million peanut butter sandwiches with the quantity of peanut butter used in Kandy Kakes each year.

4 egg whites
One 16-ounce box golden pound
    cake mix
⅔ cup water

1 cup peanut butter
½ cup powdered sugar
One 11.5-ounce bag Hershey
    milk-chocolate chips

1. Preheat the oven to 325°F.
2. Beat the egg whites until fluffy.
3. Blend the egg whites with the cake mix and water.
4. Pour tablespoon-size dollops of batter into each cup of a well-greased muffin tin. Bake for 10 minutes, or until a toothpick stuck

in center of cake comes out clean. Make five batches. Clean muffin tin for later use. Do not grease.

5. Combine the peanut butter and sugar.
6. While the pound-cake rounds cool, heat the chocolate chips in a double boiler over low heat, stirring often. You can also melt them in a microwave oven set on high for 2 minutes, stirring once halfway through the heating time.
7. When the chocolate is soft, line the bottom half of each muffin-tin cup with shortening; then use a spoon to spread a thin layer of chocolate in each cup.
8. With your fingers, spread a thin layer of peanut butter over the chocolate.
9. Place a cake round on the peanut-butter layer.
10. Spread a layer of chocolate over the top of each cake, spreading to the sides to cover the entire surface.
11. Cool in the refrigerator for 10 minutes and turn out of the tin.

- MAKES 30 CAKES

•   •   •   •

TWIN DRAGON
ALMOND COOKIES

☆ ♥ ☎ ✎ ✉ ✂ ☞

According to Main On Foods, the manufacturer and distributor of Twin Dragon Almond Cookies, the original recipe was brought to this country in 1951 by a Chinese baker who owned a small corner shop in downtown Los Angeles. That retail bakery is gone now, but its most popular product, the world's best-tasting almond cookie, is still selling big.

3 cups all-purpose flour
1 teaspoon baking soda
½ teaspoon salt
1 cup blanched almonds
1 cup granulated sugar

1½ cups lard (see Tidbits, next page)
1 teaspoon almond extract
1 egg, beaten
⅛ cup water

1. Preheat the oven to 350°F.
2. Mix the flour, baking soda, and salt.
3. In a blender, grind ½ cup blanched almonds to a fine powder. Add to the flour mixture.
4. Cream the sugar, lard, almond extract, egg, and water, and add to the dry mixture. Mix thoroughly.
5. Form into 1-inch balls and place on an ungreased cookie sheet 2 inches apart.
6. Press one of the remaining almonds into the center of each ball, while flattening it slightly with fingers.
7. Brush each cookie lightly with beaten egg.
8. Bake for 20 minutes, or until cookies are light brown around edges.

• MAKES 2 DOZEN COOKIES

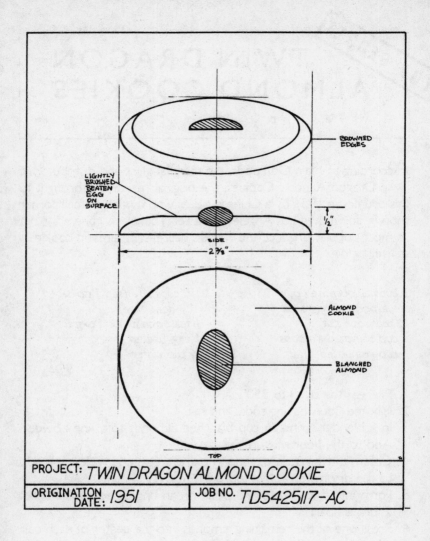

BROWNED EDGES

LIGHTLY BRUSHED BEATEN EGG ON SURFACE

$\frac{1}{2}$"

SIDE

$2\frac{3}{8}$"

ALMOND COOKIE

BLANCHED ALMOND

TOP

PROJECT: *TWIN DRAGON ALMOND COOKIE*

ORIGINATION DATE: *1951*

JOB NO. *TD5425117-AC*

TIDBITS

If your daily allowance of lard will be exceeded by this recipe, feel free to substitute vegetable shortening.

•　•　•　•　•

WENDY'S CHILI

☆   ♥   ☎   ✎   ✉   ✂   ☞

In 1969, at the ripe old age of thirty-seven, R. David Thomas left a job at Arthur Treacher's Fish & Chips to open the first Wendy's at 257 E. Broad Street in downtown Columbus, Ohio. Only three years later Thomas began franchising the Wendy's concept, and by the end of its first nine years, Wendy's International had dotted the country with more than 1,000 units.

Thomas has served this chili since day one. The recipe has changed a bit over the years, but the chili you'll taste here is a clone of Wendy's current recipe. Try topping it with freshly grated cheese and chopped onion, extras that you can request at the restaurant.

2 pounds ground beef
One 29-ounce can tomato sauce
One 29-ounce can kidney beans
    (with liquid)
One 29-ounce can pinto beans
    (with liquid)
1 cup diced onion (1 medium
    onion)

½ cup diced green chili (2 chilies)
¼ cup diced celery (1 stalk)
3 meduim tomatoes, chopped
2 teaspoons cumin powder
3 tablespoons chili powder
1½ teaspoons black pepper
2 teaspoons salt
2 cups water

1. Brown the ground beef in a skillet over medium heat; drain off the fat.
2. Using a fork, crumble the cooked beef into pea-size pieces.
3. In a large pot, combine the beef plus all the remaining ingredients, and bring to a simmer over low heat. Cook, stirring every 15 minutes, for 2 to 3 hours.

• MAKES ABOUT 12 SERVINGS

Variations

For spicier chili, add ½ teaspoon more black pepper.

For much spicier chili, add 1 teaspoon black pepper and 1 tablespoon cayenne pepper.

And for a real stomach stinger, add 5 or 6 sliced jalapeño peppers to the pot.

Leftovers can be frozen for several months.

• • • •

WENDY'S FROSTY

☆　♥　☎　✎　✉　✂　☞

The founder of Wendy's International, R. David Thomas, named the restaurant he established in 1969 after his eight-year-old daughter, Melinda Lou, who was nicknamed Wendy by her brother and sisters. Wendy says, "Dad wanted a name that was easy to remember and that was an all-American mug." Wendy is grown up now, but Dave Thomas still uses her eight-year-old freckle-faced likeness on his restaurant signs. He remembers that his daughter was very embarrassed by the exposure. Thomas told *People* magazine, "I'm not sure I would do it again."

Wendy's International now operates some 3,800 restaurants in 49 states and 24 countries overseas, racking up sales of more than $3 billion a year. Wendy's restaurants have served the now-famous Frosty since 1969. In 1991 an astounding 17.5 million gallons of the frozen confection were served worldwide.

¾ cup milk
¼ cup chocolate-drink powder
　(Nestlé Quik is best)
4 cups vanilla ice cream

1. Combine all of the ingredients in a blender. Blend on medium speed until creamy. Stir if necessary.
2. If too thin, freeze the mixture in the blender or in cups until thicker.

• Makes 2 drinks

•　•　•　•

YOO-HOO
CHOCOLATE DRINK

☆   ♥   ☎   ✎   ✉   ✂   ☛

In the early 1920s the Olivieri family had found modest success with a small company named Yoo-Hoo that produced and sold Yoo-Hoo fresh-squeezed fruit juice. But Mr. Natale Olivieri thought that adding a chocolate drink to his line would increase his sales dramatically.

A New York company named Marvis was already selling a chocolate drink, but it contained many chemicals used as preservatives. To be consistent with his policy of using only natural ingredients, Mr. Olivieri had to develop a way of bottling the chocolate drink without using additives. His solution came one day when he was helping his wife bottle her homemade tomato sauce. He noticed that she was using heat to keep the tomato sauce from spoiling, so he prepared six bottles of chocolate drink the same way. After a while, three of the six bottles spoiled, but three others remained perfect, leading him to believe he was on to something. That was Yoo-Hoo's beginning. And it didn't take long for the drink to become so successful that a major bottler began to distribute the product.

The Yoo-Hoo fresh-fruit drinks are gone now, but the high-quality chocolate-milk drink is still made from the finest cocoas available. And today it comes in two other flavors—strawberry and coconut. Sales continue to grow.

½ cup chocolate-drink powder   1½ cups nonfat dry milk
    (Nestlé Quik is best)   3 cups water

1. Mix all of the contents in a blender for about 30 seconds.
2. Refrigerate until cool.

• MAKES 2 DRINKS

• • • •

T R A D E M A R K S

"*Aunt Jemima*" and "*Aunt Jemima Syrup*" are registered trademarks of the Quaker Oats Company.

"*Ben & Jerry's Ice Cream*" is a registered trademark of Ben & Jerry's Homemade, Inc.

"*Cracker Jack*" and "*Borden*" are registered trademarks of Borden, Inc.

"*Almond Roca*" and "*Brown and Haley*" are registered trademarks of Brown and Haley, Inc.

"*Whopper*" and "*Burger King*" are registered trademarks of the Burger King Corporation.

"*Carl's Famous Star*" and "*Carl's Jr.*" are registered trademarks of Carl Karcher Enterprises.

"*Chick-fil-A*" is a registered trademark of Chick-fil-A, Inc.

"*Blizzard*," "*Orange Julius*," and "*Dairy Queen*" are registered trademarks of International Dairy Queen, Inc.

"*Hardee's*" is a registered trademark of Hardee's Food Systems, Inc.

"*Heath*" is a registered trademark of L. S. Heath & Sons, Inc.

"*Skor*," "*Reese's*," and "*Hershey*" are registered trademarks of Hershey Foods Corporation.

"*Twinkie*" and "*Hostess*" are registered trademarks of Continental Baking Company.

"*Double-Double*" and "*In-N-Out*" are registered trademarks of In-N-Out, Inc.

"*Jumbo Jack*" and "*Jack-in-the-Box*" are registered trademarks of Jack-in-the-Box, Inc.

"*Kahlúa*" is a registered trademark of the Hiram-Walker Group.

"*Soft Batch*" and "*Keebler*" are registered trademarks of the Keebler Company.

"*KFC*," "*Original Recipe*" Chicken, "*Enchirito*," and "*Taco Bell*" are registered trademarks of PepsiCo.

"*Long John Silver's*" is a registered trademark of Jerrico, Inc.

"*Twix*," "*Snickers*," and "*M&M/Mars*" are registered trademarks of M&M/Mars, Inc.

"*Big Mac*," "*Egg McMuffin*," "*McD.L.T.*," "*McLean Deluxe*," and "*McDonald's*" are registered trademarks of McDonald's Corporation.

"*Peanut Butter Dream Bar*" and "*Mrs. Fields*" are registered trademarks of Mrs. Fields, Inc.

"*Lorna Doone*" and "*Nabisco*" are registered trademarks of Nabisco Brands, Inc.

BIBLIOGRAPHY

BOAS, MAX, AND CHAIN, STEVE. *Big Mac: The Unauthorized Story of McDonald's.* New York: New American Library, 1976.

CATHY, S. TRUETT. *It's Easier to Succeed Than to Fail.* Nashville, Tenn.: Oliver-Nelson Publishers, 1989.

COHEN, BEN, AND GREENFIELD, JERRY. *Ben & Jerry's Homemade Ice Cream and Dessert Book.* New York: Workman Publishing, 1987.

CROCKER, BETTY. *Betty Crocker Cookbook.* New York: Prentice Hall Press, 1986.

FIELDS, DEBRA. *One Smart Cookie.* New York: Simon & Schuster, 1987.

HAUGHTON, NATALIE. *365 Great Chocolate Desserts.* New York: HarperCollins Publishers, 1991.

KROC, RAY. *Grinding It Out: The Making of McDonald's.* Chicago: Contemporary Books, 1985.

LOVE, JOHN. *McDonald's: Behind the Arches.* New York: Bantam, 1986.

PILLSBURY COMPANY STAFF. *Pillsbury Chocolate Lovers Cookbook.* New York: Doubleday, 1991.

PILLSBURY COMPANY. *Pillsbury Cookbook: The All-Purpose Companion for Today's Cook.* New York: Doubleday, 1991.

POUNDSTONE, WILLIAM. *Big Secrets: The Uncensored Truth About All Sorts of Stuff You Are Never Supposed to Know.* New York: William Morrow, 1983.

ROMBAUER, IRMA S. *The Joy of Cooking,* vol. 2. New York: New American Library, 1974.

SUNSET MAGAZINE AND BOOK EDITORS. *Easy Basics for Good Cooking.* Menlo Park, Calif.: Sunset Books, 1982.

THOMAS, DAVE. *Dave's Way.* New York: Putnam, 1991.

I N D E X